The Important Books

Children's Picture Books as Art and Literature

Joseph Stanton

THE SCARECROW PRESS, INC.
Lanham, Maryland • Toronto • Oxford
2005

SCARECROW PRESS, INC.

Published in the United States of America
by Scarecrow Press, Inc.
A wholly owned subsidary of
The Rowman & Littlefield Publishing Group, Inc.
4501 Forbes Boulevard, Suite 200, Lanham, Maryland 20706
www.scarecrowpress.com

PO Box 317
Oxford
OX2 9RU, UK

British Library Cataloguing in Publication Information Available

Library of Congress Cataloging-in-Publication Data

Stanton, Joseph, 1949–
    The important books : children's picture books as art and literature /
Joseph Stanton.
        p. cm.
    Includes bibliographical references.
    ISBN 0-8108-5176-8 (pbk. : alk. paper)
    1. Illustrated children's books—United States. 2. Illustration of
books—United States—20th century. I. Title.

NC975.S83 2005
741.6'42'0973—dc22

                                                              2005010487

For my children,
Susan and David,
my longtime teammates in the
reading of picture books

Contents

Acknowledgments   vii

1   Introduction   1

2   "Goodnight Nobody": Comfort and the Vast Dark in the
Picture-Poems of Margaret Wise Brown and Her Collaborators   7

3   Straight Man and Clown in the Picture Books of
Arnold Lobel   19

4   The Cycle of the Seasons in Hall and Cooney's *Ox-Cart Man*   27

5   The New York City Picture Books of Maurice Sendak   37

6   Dashing Heroes and Eccentric Families in William Joyce's
Picture Sagas of Our Common Culture   53

7   Surrealism and the Strange Tale in the Picture Books of
Chris Van Allsburg   73

Acknowledgments

Versions of some of the discussions presented in this book have appeared as follows. Comments on Margaret Wise Brown appeared in *The Lion and the Unicorn* (Johns Hopkins University Press, December 1990); on Arnold Lobel in *Journal of American Culture* (Popular Press, summer 1994); on Maurice Sendak in *Children's Literature* (Yale University Press, 2000); on William Joyce in *Visual Communication: Rhetorics and Technologies* (Rochester Institute of Technology, 2005); on Chris Van Allsburg in *Children's Literature* (Yale University Press, 1996); and on the nature of picture-book art in general in *American Art* (The Smithsonian, 1998).

Early drafts of many of these essays were also included in proceedings volumes and humanities guides for the Biennial Conference on Literature and Hawaii's Children.

The cover illustration is from *George Shrinks* copyright © 1985 by William Joyce and is used by permission of HarperCollins Publisher. All rights reserved.

Excerpts from *Old and New Poems* by Donald Hall copyright © 1990 by Donald Hall are used by permission of Houghton Mifflin and Company. All rights reserved.

Excerpts from *Ox-Cart Man* by Donald Hall copyright © 1979 are used by permission of Viking Penguin, A Division of Penguin Young Readers Group, A Member of Penguin Group (USA) Inc., 345 Hudson Street, New York, NY 10014. All rights reserved.

Introduction

This volume takes its title from a beautifully basic and oddly moving picture book with words by Margaret Wise Brown and images by Leonard Weisgard. Brown and Weisgard's *The Important Book* fulfills an elementary mission for small children and the adults who read with them. In the manner of a here-and-now book it confirms some basic facts about the world through simple and direct statements, telling us, for instance, that "the important thing about an apple is that it is round," but this book does more than confirm simple facts. It is primarily a work of art, a lyrically simple picture poem about the things of the world. The value it has for the child-and-parent audiences who read and reread it night after night goes beyond the very slight educational value its little cluster of facts has to offer.

The children's picture book is an important form of literary-visual art. To properly appreciate the best examples of the form, however, we need to dispose of some of the assumptions that have tended to obscure this genre's achievements. While I am most intent on praising those picture books that are distinguished by some degree of originality in both word and image, many of my claims also apply to illustrated versions of abridged antique texts, such as the endless renderings of the tales of the Brothers Grimm.

First, the importance of pictures in children's books is not primarily pedagogical. Pictures make books more desirable and interesting, but they do not necessarily contribute directly to the improvement of "decoding skills." To serve as aids to comprehension, picture-book art has no need to be as striking as it routinely is.

Second, it must be realized that the better-illustrated fictions for small children are not "dumbed-down" versions of the kinds of fictions available in adult novels. In reality, the plots of many of the best children's picture books involve radical experiments in such features as "excess, indeterminacy, and boundary breaking," to use David Lewis's terms (Lewis, 131). Perhaps the best way to restate Lewis's point is to say that picture books are often more poetic than prosaic. The relative brevity of the picture-book form allows for intense manipulation of forms (and reader expectations about forms) without the danger of a loss of coherence that might result from such manipulations in a novel-length narrative. But sophistication in the picture-book genre should not be equated with abstruseness. A sophisticated picture book is not necessarily harder to understand than an unsophisticated one. With regard to both poems and pictures, the greatest works are sometimes the most beautifully simple. A key reason why both subtlety and simplicity are possible is the double nature of the form. The picture-book maker can make the presentation of simple words sophisticated by the way the images are handled. Likewise, subtle use of words can add nuance to the simplest of images. The rich prospects for counterpoint, interplay, and irony made available through the double nature of the form are the wonderful and too seldom acknowledged artistic advantages of the genre. The images do not merely illustrate the words; the words do not merely explain the images. Image and word can reverberate in each other's company to surprising effect.

Third, the audience for children's picture books is routinely misunderstood by commentators. The audience is only half children. More often than not the picture book must appeal to both the parent and the child in equal measure. The parent is, in fact, more crucial to the marketplace circumstances that spur the ongoing development of the form; after all, it is usually the parent who selects the picture book at a bookstore or library. The unusual partnership between parent and child that is intimately involved in the demand for the form has created a context in which a special kind of excellence can prosper: Picture-book writers and artists cannot afford to bore or mystify either parent or child, and the region where the delight of both meets is a very special place that only the very best picture-book makers can reach. When a picture book fully succeeds, it unites its pairs of readers in a special bond. Because the children's picture book is designed to provide the context for an intimate transaction involving the imaginations of both parent and child, there is a social value to the form that lends a special poignancy to the pleasure it provides.

When Everyone Was Fast Asleep by Tomie dePaola, one of the most widely popular picture-book makers, is a masterful bedtime story. Like Margaret Wise Brown and Clement Hurd's *Goodnight Moon*, it takes the dark of night and the drift into sleep as central motifs. Nothing much happens here—two children go to bed and dream a lovely pageant—but beyond and within the simplicity of the book lies a subtle artistry. The night sky becomes a fog maiden whose long, flowing hair, robe, and scarf embody evening clouds. A hint of danger gives a sharp edge to the adventures of this soft dream. The fog maiden is a gigantic, page-filling presence, and her cat messenger also has a cloudlike immensity, but the narration makes clear at every point that the children are in kindly hands. As the reader-viewer of the book proceeds, it becomes apparent that the spatial compositions the vast maiden and her cat inhabit are at least as important as their involvement in the tale's plot. The stylized pictures are dreams in their own right that simultaneously counterpoint and elucidate the dream events conveyed by the words.

DePaola's *When Everyone Was Fast Asleep* provides an interesting example of an adult reference that does not interfere with the pleasure of younger consumers. In the midst of a dream-theater production, a scene involving a lion and a gypsy becomes a witty recasting of Henri Rousseau's painting *The Sleeping Gypsy*. This art-historical appropriation is handled with a disarming smoothness of transition and consistency of tone that easily persuades us that Rousseau's gypsy and lion could call dePaola's book their home.

The gentle ease of dePaola's allusion could be contrasted with Maurice Sendak's uneasy but equally witty insertion of an image of Mozart into *Outside Over There*. But the case of Sendak—in many respects the greatest contemporary master of the picture-book form—raises a crucial issue for the still-developing art of the picture book. Guardians of children's literature are sometimes quick to condemn works, even those by masters of the form, that fall outside the ready grasp of the "average" child. Sendak, in particular, has been criticized for the pride he takes in achieving an adult audience that is unambiguously attracted to his books for its own pleasure, regardless of whether these adults have children with whom they can share them. It should, however, be understood that picture books that appeal primarily to sophisticated sensibilities will naturally be part of the mix as this compelling genre continues to develop. Sometimes, as was the case with the initial response to the publication of Sendak's *Where the Wild Things Are*, children are capable of appreciating the greatness of a compelling original work more readily than many adults.

Classic pieces by artist-writers such as dePaola and Sendak help make a case for the reversal of the usual hierarchy and provide some support for the claim that the best picture books are sometimes, perhaps often, more interesting works of art than the best novels (of both juvenile and adult varieties). One symptom of this reversal is the best-seller status of children's picture books, such as Sendak's *Outside Over There*. Another symptom is the remarkable following gained by such adult picture books as Nick Bantock's *Griffin and Sabine* series.

What I am pointing out is not "the death of the novel." (Critics have been talking about the death of the novel since the 1950s without making any dent in the number of novels published.) What I am speaking of is the coming-of-age of the picture book. Anyone who needs further confirmation of this phenomenon would do well to read *The Picture Book Comes of Age* by Joseph Schwarcz, whose essay on Ezra Jack Keats's *Whistle for Willie* makes clear that even the simplest picture books can be deft and complexly satisfying works of art.

It should hardly be surprising that the picture-book genre is artistically among the best products America's publishers have to offer. Novels can by definition be nothing more than prosaic, and, unfortunately, most recent volumes of poetry can be described the same way. A picture book, conceived in our time, has, above and beyond its literary resources, the vast repertoire of compositional and coloristic strategies from the entire history of art—European, Asian, African, and so forth—to draw upon for its visual ideas. New photographic processes have given today's picture-book artists a greatly expanded range of possibilities. No longer is the artist necessarily constrained by the limits of the mechanics of printing. Inspired by the opportunities, contemporary picture-book masters—such as Nancy Ekholm Burkert, Barbara Cooney, Leo and Diane Dillon, Tryna Schart Hyman, William Joyce, Gerald McDermott, Allen Say, Peter Sis, Chris Van Allsburg, David Wiesner, and Ed Young, to name a few—have been producing works that will undoubtedly be considered classics in the future. It is probably not an exaggeration to say that we are in the midst of a golden age of the picture book.

The picture book offers nourishment to many in our society who are starved for great art. One of the considerable advantages of the children's picture book as an art form is that it is so readily available in bookstores and libraries. It is the only form of sophisticated art that many families experience on a regular basis. Parents who might never willingly cross the threshold of a museum or art gallery or open a classic literary novel will readily consume and reconsume a great children's picture book because they assume they are doing it for the betterment of their child. As with the *ukiyo-e* woodblock prints of the Japanese Tokugawa period or the nineteenth-century illustrated English fictions of Charles Dickens, widespread distribution in no way diminishes the greatness of the best examples of the form.

WORKS CITED

Bantock, Nick. *Griffin & Sabine: An Extraordinary Correspondence.* San Francisco: Chronicle Books, 1991.

Brown, Margaret Wise. *The Important Book*. Illus. Leonard Weisgard. New York: HarperCollins, 1949.

DePaola, Tomie. *When Everyone Was Fast Asleep*. New York: Holiday House, 1976.

Keats, Ezra Jack. *Whistle for Willie*. New York: Penguin, 1970.

Lewis, David. "The Constructedness of Texts: Picture Books and the Metafictive." *Signal* 62 (May 1990): 131–46.

Schwarcz, Joseph H., and Chava Schwarz. *The Picture Book Comes of Age*. Chicago: American Library Association, 1991.

Sendak, Maurice. *Outside Over There*. New York: Harper & Row, 1981.

"Goodnight Nobody": Comfort and the Vast Dark in the Picture-Poems of Margaret Wise Brown and Her Collaborators

*M*any of the best-known books of Margaret Wise Brown and the artists with whom she collaborated are famous for the comforts they are thought to offer. It is my contention here, however, that it is the understatedly dangerous contexts in which those comforts are offered that gives them their poignancy. The kinds of dangers and comforts so quietly presented in Brown's books are, it seems to me, powerful contraries that resonate at the psychic core of the parent-child bond. The simplicity of Brown's picture-book-length poems and the rightness of the pictures that give visual form to them have made these unpretentious little books into important artistic events in the lives of innumerable children and their parents.

Two motifs that occur again and again in Brown's work are the runaway child and the child alone in the wide world. Although they obviously overlap, and the second motif is always at least partially present whenever the first motif is in operation, it is important to distinguish them because the plots driven by these two motifs polarize the parent and the child figures in two different, but strangely complementary, ways. The runaway-child plot involves the rescue or return of the child, whereas the child-alone-in-the-wide-world plot leaves the child by him- or herself while finding a satisfactory resolution within that aloneness.

Brown had a passionate yet unsentimental view of children and childhood. One important aspect of the dynamics of the parent-child relationship in Brown's books is the rebellious aggressiveness of the child. It was remarked, by Brown as well as others, that she saw herself as a child. Her identification with the child—often presented in her books as a furry or fuzzy little animal, a rabbit more often than not—was declaredly unpretentious. To underscore that her identification with children and bunnies was not sentimental, she would tell partially facetious stories about her exploits as a rabbit-hunting "beagler." As she explained to a *Life* magazine writer,

> A . . . beagler's object is to run fast enough to be in at the kill when the hounds finally catch up with their prey and, assuming that the pack has not torn the rabbit to bits before anyone can interfere, a successful beagler is rewarded by getting a rabbit's foot suitable for mounting. (Bliven, 68)

When questioned about the oddity of this hobby for one who writes of "the hopes and aspirations of small furry creatures," Brown's joking reply would be worthy of a Woody Allen: "Well, I don't especially like children either. At least not as a group. I won't let anybody get away with anything just because he is little" (68).

Despite her rigorous resistance to all tendencies that she perceived to be romanticizations of the child, she considered herself a staunch defender of the powers and prerogatives of children. Because she spent a considerable amount of time observing children and talking with them—especially during her years at Lucy Sprague Mitchell's Bank Street School—she had great confidence in her ability to understand and speak to children's needs and interests. One of the main themes of her comments about children is that adults too often underestimate them. She felt strongly that children are perceptive in ways adults are not. She saw the simplicity necessary in children's books to be a demanding discipline. In an oft-quoted line, she declared the goal of her art: "I hope I have written a book simple enough to come near to that timeless world" (Bechtel, 186). Her invention of the "noisy book" genre and her desire for strong visual and tactile qualities in books were related to her belief that children are, in some important respects, more aesthetically sophisticated than adults. Brown liked to relate an anecdote in which a teacher expressed astonishment when confronted with an abstract painting. To a teacher's "My goodness, what's that?" a child replied impatiently, "It's a picture, you dope!" (Bliven, 64).

The runaway-child motif is perhaps most famously captured by Brown in *The Runaway Bunny*. It is comforting that the little bunny who wanted to run away from his mother was answered successfully at every turn by that loving mother. There is wonderful, unqualified love in this willingness to run after the child who, of course, does not really want to get away. She will run after him simply and absolutely because he is her little bunny. The back and forth of this poetic dialogue has a marvelous cadence of real conversation that children (and their parents) enjoy. If he becomes a fish, she will become a fisherman. If he becomes a rock on a mountain, she will become a mountain climber. If he becomes a crocus in a hidden garden, she will become a gardener. And so on. There is great comfort in this. No matter what he does or how he strays, the mother's love is so great that she will find a way to be there to catch him in her arms and hug him.

But at the same time as the comfort is enforced by the mother's satisfactory and satisfying rebuttals, the child's stated plans of escape name the far reaches of the wide world. Each of the episodes sets the child dangerously apart in another way. This constant reenactment of the mother striving to reach the straying child suggests that the process could go on forever, and suggests, subtly, by the very heroism of the mother's effort, that the drama could, at some future time, end differently. The prospect of loss and abandonment is dangled again and again, and it is in the very repetition that the dangerousness of the wide world is made apparent.

Obviously, Brown's predilections have dictated the nature of this poetic dialogue, but the artist, Clement Hurd, contributes importantly to the quality and effectiveness of the finished work. His pictures for this book are of two kinds. There are the black-on-white line drawings that illustrate some of the basic details of each episode, and then for each episode there is a full-color painting, covering two facing pages, that represents the heart of the action, the mother's dramatized and in-costume readiness to rescue her baby. These large, uncaptioned pictures give Clement Hurd's painting equal partnership with Brown's writing.

Hurd's pictures reinforce and go beyond the text in several important ways. The bunnies are without facial expression and, indeed, show no signs of having mouths. This expressionlessness is an important support for Brown's unsentimental agenda. One has but to recall the many children's books with grinning animal protagonists to appreciate the importance of this expressionlessness. (In the "Curious George" books, for example, everything smiles, even fish that are about to be eaten.) Despite their lack of emotion, this mother and this child appear eminently huggable. Likewise, the gorgeous world of Clement Hurd's pictures looks deliciously soft and gloriously colorful. The richness of the colors is exciting as well as comforting. The red walls of the living room scene have, for instance, a Matisse-like intensity that will be transformed by Hurd into "the great green room" of Brown's *Goodnight Moon*. The joyous, bright magic of Hurd's pictures lights up this little book and serves to further overwhelm the dark undercurrent of potential loss; however, as I have already stressed, the repeated runnings away keep the possibility of loss alive.

In a sense, the last picture in *The Runaway Bunny* encapsulates the theme of this essay. The mother and child are sheltered in the warm food-filled comfort of their burrow, while outside the vast, indifferent universe of fields and starry skies stretches into the distance. Here again, we have an anticipation of *Goodnight Moon*, but before getting into that Brown–Hurd companion collaboration to *The Runaway Bunny*, I would like to look briefly at some other Brown collaborations where the threat of loss of the runaway is broached in other contexts.

The best of her many other books on this theme is undoubtedly *Little Lost Lamb*. It lacks the simplicity and power of *The Runaway Bunny* and does not entirely avoid sentimentality, but it is, nevertheless, one of the best of her many collaborations with Leonard Weisgard. As in the familiar parable and popular song, what we have here is a little lost lamb that has gone astray. The implausibility of the middle-of-night rescue of the lamb by the shepherd boy is somewhat of a problem in a story that is, in many respects, realistic, but the core dynamics of the lost-found motif is ultimately satisfying. There is lovely compatibility between Brown's poetical, cadenced text and Weisgard's coolly attractive paintings. As in *The Runaway Bunny* we are given a wonderful wide world whose beauty is intermingled with danger. Most writers would make the mountain lion that almost gets a chance to devour the lamb into some manner of villain; but here that skulking predator is just one of the details of a lyrically evoked landscape in which a small creature happens to be lost.

The art of Weisgard performs a role similar to the role of Hurd's art. We are moved by the positive celebration of aliveness presented by both text and picture. Nevertheless, both forms of art also provide a negative undertow: In dozens of subtle ways we are made to understand that the lamb could die in this pretty place. The shepherd boy serves as a foil to that undertow, of course, but, for all his good intentions, he is clearly a fallible protector. He would do "what a shepherd had to do," but he was well aware that it might not be enough to save the lost lamb. Part of what is touching for young readers is that the shepherd is himself a child. Young readers can, thus, identify easily with the protector as well as the runaway. The tale of the lost lamb connects with the child's (and the adult's) memories of things or people they have lost. Thus a hamster that ran away, a fish that had to be flushed, a friend that moved to another town, or even a death in the family—any such small or large sorrow would enable the reader to identify with the anxiety of the shepherd boy as he worries through the night unable to sleep.

Let me just mention in passing a few of the dozens of Brown's tales that involve variations on the runaway theme. Although her books vary considerably in quality, a surprisingly large number of them are still in print or have recently been brought back into print.

Little Chicken, another collaboration with Leonard Weisgard, was published in a format similar to that of *The Runaway Bunny* and *Goodnight Moon*.

In a reversal of *The Runaway Bunny* this story involves a parental figure that runs away and leaves the protagonist to find others to play with, which, of course, he does. The story ends with a snuggling of parent and child figures reminiscent of the concluding pages of *The Runaway Bunny*. *Home for a Bunny* and *The Golden Egg Book*, less satisfying productions, also conclude with scenes of that kind. The sentiments of these endings are, for the most part, earned by the lack of nurturing sweetness in the plots that lead up to them. Although the worlds of these lightweight books hardly seem dangerous, the protagonists are, as usual, little helpless things out there on their own. The success of Brown's treatment of aloneness and loneliness in these little books is due, in part, to the unusual amalgam of sincere sympathy and wry sense of humor that are hallmarks of her attitude toward her fictional worlds. She cares deeply about these little creatures but does not take her caring too seriously.

My last runaway example faces a seemingly more considerable threat, but the danger is mitigated by the bizarre nature of his adversaries and by the whimsical tone with which the tale is told. "A Remarkable Rabbit," a posthumously published story, is a kind of reprise of *The Runaway Bunny*. This time the runaway bunny gets captured by an odd team of villains—a frog, a snake, a worm, and a porcupine—but this peculiarly menacing gang cannot keep him down. He gets away by slyly outwitting the bad guys. He is, after all, a "remarkable rabbit."

The best and most famous of Brown's child-alone-in-the-wide-world plots is *Goodnight Moon*. I expect to hear some objections. It might be pointed out that this child is neither alone nor out in the wide world. *Goodnight Moon* is, in fact, renowned for its cozy comforts. The child is protected by "the quiet old lady whispering 'hush'" and sheltered by "the great green room." It is my contention here, however, that this book has been so profoundly moving to so many children and adults precisely because Brown poetically invokes, with the considerable help of Hurd's pictures, both a comforting interior space and an overwhelming exterior space. I can think of no other book that provides the kind of experience this one does, although it has had numerous imitators.

The book embodies an uncomplicated, yet subtly modulated, process. Preparatory to going to sleep, a child, illustrated as a bunny in the same style that was used in *The Runaway Bunny*, says goodnight to the world of his bedroom, as well as to the world in general. As these goodnights proceed the room gradually darkens, from page to page, while the moon-filled sky gradually brightens. Part of the magic here is the result of the nature of the voice that speaks the goodnights. Unlike most books in the goodnight genre—a genre that has become an industry, in part because of the legendary popularity of Brown's classic—*Goodnight Moon* does not feature a parental figure helping a child to say his or her goodnights. Here the child's point of view is all we have. The child has complete authority here. Everything in this universe revolves around the child as the central human presence, and this presence names its universe.

There is a problem here, however. The voice speaking in *Goodnight Moon* does not sound like the voice of a child. It is a knowing voice, a whimsical voice, a voice that sees and comprehends what the child sees and understands in the universe the book creates. It is, of course, the omniscient voice of Margaret Wise Brown at its poetic best. Brown has found here a powerful vehicle for her voice. The oracular nature of this authorial naming of the universe taps into the power of a basic type of myth that has "comforted" people of all ages. It is, in essence, a creation myth in a kind of end-of-the-world (rather than beginning-of-the-world) pattern. Of course, the end of the world here is merely a saying goodnight to the world, but the mythic weight of this ritualistic naming of things is implicit in the satisfactions this simple little book provides.

The bright pictures of Clement Hurd are key to the success of *Goodnight Moon*. Brown worked closely with Hurd on the conceptualization of the pictures. Because she was an important editor as well as a highly in-demand author, she was in a better position to genuinely collaborate than are most children's book writers. In addition, Hurd and many of the artists Brown worked with were her close personal friends.

There is an enormous amount that could be said about the interface of words and images in this book. I will limit myself to a few observations. In the pictures, as in the poem, the child is the center of this universe. Although the child-bunny is in bed throughout the book, he is the active protagonist around which the action revolves. He changes position and what he is looking at from one frame to the next. His shifts are not highly dramatic. Sometimes he is partially under the covers; sometimes he is sitting or crouching on top of them; but everything in the scene is clearly oriented around him and what he is looking at. His stance always relates in some way to what is being named. By contrast, "the quiet old lady whispering 'hush'" is a virtual statue. She is sometimes absent, with her knitting equipment left on her rocker, but when she is present she is always in the same position, one hand on her lap and the other raised to her mouth to signal the quiet she demands. It is significant that she is described simply as an "old lady," with no indication of any connection to the child. The child is essentially alone in the world of this book. The old woman is not treated as a parent or even as a person. She is just one of the features of the landscape. The child sits alone in a universe that extends from delightfully trivial details such as "a comb and a brush and a bowl full of mush" to the vast outside that includes stars, air, and even the whimsically puzzling "nobody."

Although the old woman stays put, other creatures of the room move about in ways that delight young consumers of this book. The kittens play themselves into several positions and, most delightful of all, there is a mouse that changes position radically from one frame to the next. The changing position of the tiny mouse serves as a "find-me" game for young readers, yet even the mouse seems to be saying goodnight to many of the named things. The stance of the mouse plays a kind of musical counterpoint to the stance of the child-bunny.

It is with regard to light and dark that I would like to tie together the strands of my interpretation of *Goodnight Moon*. In this reverse creation myth we meet the child in the midst of his world of things—his pictures, his toys, his socks, his old woman whispering "hush," and so forth. As the room darkens the things are gradually lost in a dark that is only slightly mitigated by the nightlight inside the toy house and a lingering fire in the fireplace. What becomes dominant in the concluding pictures is the moon and the sky that has changed to a bright blue to give us a sense of the brightness of a moonlit night once interior house lights are dimmed. Although the now familiar but dimmed details of the room are overwhelmed visually by this marvelous evocation of the moonstruck night, the child and his point of view are still strongly present in the speaking voice of the poem. He is securely present in the center of his universe, yet he is completely alone in that godlike eminence. The child is regarding, at the last, a vast dark of "noises everywhere" in which the child is alone but unafraid. The child is finally lost in his sleep while the universe gleams on without him.

Similar instances of the child-alone-in-the-wide-world motif recur often in Brown's books. The motif can be established in single scenes in books that are preoccupied with other motifs. For instance, the concluding scene in *Little Lost Lamb*, in which the boy is returning from the mountain with the rescued lamb in his arms, shows boy and lamb against a backdrop of a most impressive vast dark. We are told that the boy "sang to the night" and are given a repetition of the simple shepherd's song that had also been presented at the beginning of the tale. The feel of this scene is similar in many respects to that of the conclusion of *Goodnight Moon*. The shepherd boy's singing to the night is roughly parallel to the child-bunny's naming of his universe.

In Brown's lovely collaboration with Jean Charlot, *A Child's Goodnight Book*, the voice speaking a poetic goodnight takes an adult point of view that names children as among the things that will sleep. It all adds up to a prayer to God on behalf of all "small things that have no words." God, invoked as a protector, is asked to "guard with tenderness" all the helpless little ones. Although this poem does not avoid sentimentality, it provides another way for Brown to eloquently poetize the vulnerability of the child and the childlike. The final Charlot picture, in which two angels have gathered up into a blanket all the helpless small things—a jumble of two children, a lamb, a fish, a bird, a rabbit, a dragonfly, and a cat—may seem rather sweet for some tastes; however, the attractive and dignified cadence of the poem and the delicate power of Charlot's picture make it difficult to resist this bedtime picture song for those at the mercy of the vast dark world of night.

One more instance of the child-alone motif, *The Little Island*, provides a useful example of how this motif need not be restricted to the night and darkness contexts I have discussed thus far. This example of another of Brown's best books was a collaboration with Leonard Weisgard for which she wrote under the pseudonym Golden MacDonald. There are two child surrogates in *The Little Island*: the island itself and a small cat that comes to the island on a boat. Most of the book involves the kind of naming of the universe that we observed in *Goodnight Moon*. Again, naming has a kind of incantatory effect that surrounds the protagonist with a world through a quasi-mythic recitation. Here, however, the world is presented in fairly realistic detail. This text could, in fact, be used to help children get some sense of how and why seasons change. The way this book asks its readers to experience the passing of time as the pages turn is parallel to the way *Goodnight Moon* asks the reader to experience the bedtime hour.

The little island's situation as a child alone in the wide world is given a kind of resolution that is explained to the kitten. (This is a departure from the pattern of *Goodnight Moon*, where the child's aloneness remains unacknowledged and unexplained.) The kitten recognizes that he himself is "a little fur Island in the air," and eventually comes to the realization that any island is also a part of the land because "all land is one land under the sea." This unity of all things must be accepted on "Faith." Thus the underlying truth that "no man is an island" must remain *entirely* underlying. The day-to-day life of the island is a life lived alone. The important fact of the island's connectedness is of no obvious practical value but is simply a treasured realization that the island hugs to itself. The closing lines of the book make clear the balanced resolution: "And it was good to be a little Island. A part of the world and a world of its own all surrounded by the bright blue sea."

Weisgard's pictures are lovely and loving depictions of the various aspects of the Little Island described in Brown's words. Weisgard had spent time with Brown in one of her houses on a small island off the coast of Maine. The view from Brown's house, which she called the "Only House," overlooked an expanse of sea including a tiny fragment of rock and grass, the little island that inspired the book (Marcus, 163–65). The quiet beauty of such places is one of the themes of the book. The close friendship of Brown and Weisgard is evident in the harmonious compatibility of their visions. His landscapes provide wonderful counterparts to her words. The sense of the place is equally vivid and equally simple in the two forms of art. Both writer and artist achieve sophisticated effects with a minimum of strokes.

Although Brown's books deal with many concerns beyond the two motifs I have examined here, I think it is obvious that the runaway-child and the child-alone-in-the-wide-world motifs were important to Brown because they generate stories that speak to the basic needs of children (including such grown-up children as Brown herself and the parents who buy and borrow her books). The impulse of the child in Brown's books is almost always toward independence, but the independence of small creatures is always problematic. These two motifs present those problems in complementary ways. Brown cherished both possibilities: The rescue of the runaway by a loved one is a marvelously satisfying outcome, but so too is the child who experiences aloneness yet remains unafraid. Perhaps the latter motif was dominant for Brown; one of her last published books before her death was *Mister Dog: The Dog Who Belonged to Himself.*

Throughout her brief life (she died at forty-two of a complication in a routine operation) Brown was a confidently independent individual, much like her protagonists. Her rambunctious, wittily mischievous, self-reliant style of life was more than a little unusual for her time or any time. She enjoyed being alone—she once told a reporter that her hobby was "privacy"—yet she also had a wide circle of close friends. She never achieved the success she had hoped for as a writer of poetry or fiction for the adult market, but she made the best of her own unique form of literary art—a form of prose poem for children's picture books that could achieve a kind of eloquence for which simplicity of statement was a precondition. That this kind of eloquence requires pictures to realize its full expression is a special feature of that eloquence rather than a limitation.

It could be argued that the children's picture book is, in certain respects, one of society's most valuable forms of art. It is a form of art both literary and graphic that parents can hold in their hands to share with their youngest and, therefore, most fragile of children. The intimate transaction between parent, child, and picture book is one that Brown appears to have understood well. She found ways to make that core interconnectedness—and the core

aloneness that is the other side of that coin—the primary focus of her art and
the art of the collaborators she brought into her projects. The example of
her best works shows picture-book makers that the most primary of subjects
for picture books, the parent-child bond, can be addressed directly if one has
the wisdom and the wit to achieve genuine simplicity.

WORKS CITED

Bechtel, Louise Seaman. "Margaret Wise Brown, 'Laureate of the Nursery.'" *The Horn Book Magazine*, June 1958: 173–86.
Bliven, Bruce, Jr. "Child's Best Seller." *Life*, December 2, 1946: 59–68.
Brown, Margaret Wise. *A Child's Good Night Book*. Illus. Jean Charlot. New York: W. R. Scott, 1950.
———. *The Golden Egg Book*. Illus. Leonard Weisgard. New York: Simon & Schuster, 1947. (There is also a 1962 edition with pictures by Lilian Obligado. The Weisgard version was lavishly decorated with wildflowers because Brown loved wildflowers and felt children would, too.)
———. *Goodnight Moon*. Illus. Clement Hurd. New York: Harper, 1947.
———. *Home for a Bunny*. Illus. Garth Williams. New York: Simon & Schuster, 1956.
———. *Little Chicken*. Illus. Leonard Weisgard. New York: Harper, 1943.
———. (pseudonym Golden MacDonald). *The Little Island*. Illus. Leonard Weisgard. Garden City, NY: Doubleday, 1946. (This book won the Caldecott Medal.)
———. (pseudonym Golden MacDonald). *Little Lost Lamb*. Illus. Leonard Weisgard. Garden City, NY: Doubleday, 1945.
———. *Mister Dog: The Dog Who Belonged to Himself*. Illus. Garth Williams. New York: Simon & Schuster, 1952.
———. "A Remarkable Rabbit." *Once Upon a Time in a Pigpen and Three Other Stories*. Illus. Ann Strugell. Reading, MA: Addison-Wesley, 1980.
———. *The Runaway Bunny*. Illus. Clement Hurd. New York: Harper, 1942. (When Hurd repainted some of the pictures for a new 1972 edition, he made the colors more intense and Matisse-like.)
Marcus, Leonard. *Margaret Wise Brown: Awakened by the Moon*. Boston: Beacon, 1992.

OTHER WORKS OF INTEREST

Bader, Barbara. "Margaret Wise Brown." *American Picturebooks from Noah's Art to the Beast Within*. New York: Macmillan, 1976. 252–64.
Brown, Margaret Wise. *Big Red Barn*. Illus. Rosella Hartman. New York: W. R. Scott, 1956.

————. *Christmas in the Barn.* Illus. Barbara Cooney. New York: Crowell, 1952. (The pictures are wonderful. Cooney was one of the best.)

————. *David's Little Indian.* Illus. Remy Charlip. Birmingham, AL: Hopscotch, 1989.

————. *Nibble Nibble: Poems for Children.* Illus. Leonard Weisgard. New York: W. R. Scott, 1959.

————. *The Noisy Book.* Illus. Leonard Weisgard. New York: W. R. Scott, 1939. (The seven books in the Noisy Book series were considered by many to be Brown's and Weisgard's most innovative contributions to the picture book genre. Everything in these books revolves around what a little dog named Muffin could and could not hear. Among other things, the series showed how questions could be used to involve small children in the matter of a book.)

————. *SHHhhhh. . . . BANG: A Whispering Book.* Illus. Robert De Veyrac. New York: Harper, 1943.

————. *Two Little Trains.* Illus. Jean Charlot. New York: W. R. Scott, 1949. (Maurice Sendak has praised this book as "a little masterpiece" and a "miracle of bookmaking." See article cited below.)

Galbraith, Mary. "'Goodnight Nobody' Revisited: Using an Attachment Perspective to Study Picture Books about Bedtime." *Children's Literature Association Quarterly* 23, No. 4 (1998–1999): 172–80. (Galbraith sees the child-alone aspect of *Goodnight Moon* and other bedtime books as evidence of a considerable human problem. She argues that the small child's need for constant attachment to the parent is blocked by the "dogmas of European-American parenting" that make it "mandatory for children to sleep alone in a separate room" [173].) The title of Galbraith's article makes reference to an earlier version of my Margaret Wise Brown essay. My essay appeared in *The Lion and the Unicorn: A Critical Journal of Children's Literature* 14, No. 2 (December 1990): 66–76.

Marcus, Leonard. "The Legend of Margaret Wise Brown." *Publishers Weekly* 22 (July 1983): 74–76.

————. *The Making of Goodnight Moon.* New York: HarperCollins, 1997.

————. *Margaret Wise Brown: Awakened by the Moon.* Boston: Beacon, 1992. (This is an excellent and valuable biography. Although I did not have the benefit of this volume when I was doing research for my Brown essay in the late 1980s, I did catch a small glimpse of some of this material in the form of Marcus's *Publisher's Weekly* article cited above.)

Sendak, Maurice. "Margaret Wise Brown and Jean Charlot." *Caldecott & Co.: Notes on Books & Pictures.* New York: Farrar, 1988.

· 3 ·

Straight Man and Clown in the Picture Books of Arnold Lobel

$\mathcal{W}$ith the death of Arnold Lobel at the age of only fifty-four in 1987 America lost one of its best and most popular children's book creators. "Easy readers," books designed for beginning readers, seldom win the major children's literature awards because they are usually thought to contain too few words to establish the literary distinction necessary to win the Newbery and too many words to allow for the illustrational distinction needed to merit the Caldecott. Lobel's efforts as an artist-writer of easy readers have, however, been singled out for both Caldecott and Newbery honors, as well as for numerous other awards. The universality and whimsicality of Lobel's tales contribute to their popularity, as do the inexpensive standardized format and effective marketing employed by Harper & Row (now known as HarperCollins) for all its easy-reader paperbacks. It is safe to say that every public library in America (and a multitude of homes) is in possession of well-worn copies of I Can Read books by Arnold Lobel. The Frog and Toad series is by far the most popular, but his books with grasshopper, owl, mouse, and elephant protagonists also have wide appeal.

In a number of the most characteristic books of Arnold Lobel the central personalities are handled in one of three ways: Either there is a solitary, highly emotional (one might even say foolish) individual or a solitary reasonable individual, or there are two complementary personalities, one more foolish and the other relatively more reasonable. It would be tempting to call the foolish personality childish or childlike as opposed to the presumably more adult demeanor of the reasonable personality, but Lobel would be quick to remind us that children and adults are not, at bottom, different kinds of persons. Adults and children have the same kinds of hopes, fears, and foolishnesses even though the details of what they are concerned about may differ. Lobel pointed out in a 1971 interview in *The Lion and the Unicorn* that "a child's sense of humor and an adult's sense of humor are rather the same. And if you don't have a sense of humor when you're a child, you're not going to have one when you're an adult" (Natov and DeLuca, 84).

It might be expected that the punch line of this chapter would have to be an argument for the superiority of the stories that favor the reasonable perspectives as against the emotional, but I find myself unable to judge one of the three strategies consistently preferable in either human or artistic terms. Thus the Frog and Toad books (where reason and emotion are somewhat reconciled and held in balance), *Owl at Home* (where the foolish one does without reasonable advice), and *Grasshopper on the Road* (where a solitary reasonable protagonist is featured) are all equally satisfying.

It should be remembered that the most interesting characters in Lobel's work are like real people in that they have hints of both reasonableness and foolishness in their personalities. For instance, even the quite reasonably avuncular Uncle Elephant is a bit of a silly in some of his ways. Thus I should provide advance warning that my thesis cannot be insisted upon too rigorously.

Most of my examples will be drawn from the books Lobel did for Harper & Row's I Can Read series. The format of that series proved to be perfect for his talents. These collections of brief stories encouraged experimentation; no one story had to stand alone. Lobel could indulge his whimsical imagination freely in this format without fear that the eccentricity of any particular episode would endanger the project. There is, by contrast, a timidness to some of the single-story picture books he did before he hit his stride in the I Can Read books. His use of a giant and flocks of fairies in *Giant John*, for instance, seems to have been motivated by a desire to give his story the appearance of a fairy tale. Although the plot of this picture book bears some resemblance to certain Frog and Toad plots, readers cannot identify with the unimaginatively conceived giant to the same extent they can with Frog and Toad. The whimsy is there, but Lobel has failed to make it work for him, due largely to the reliance on hackneyed and unappealing characters. The I Can Read format, which freed him from having to fit each individual story into conventionally marketable formulas, and his maturing ability to draw animals in a style obviously influenced by Beatrix Potter enabled him to develop appealing animal characters well suited to his whimsical narrative tendencies.

The Frog and Toad books are, of course, central to my argument. The overwrought emotions of Toad are fully apparent in the first of these books, *Frog and Toad Are Friends*, published in 1970. In "Spring," Toad stubbornly refuses to get up from his winter's sleep until tricked into it by Frog. In "The

Story," Toad puts himself through bizarre agonies in an unsuccessful effort to think of a story. In "A Lost Button," Toad's excessive emotionality is made abundantly clear in the temper tantrum he throws because of a lost button. In "A Swim," Toad poutingly refuses to come out of the swimming hole because he does not want anyone to see his ridiculous bathing suit. In "The Letter," Toad needlessly and routinely plunges himself into melancholy because he never gets any letters. Toad in all these stories shows himself to be willful and self-preoccupied. Frog is ever the commonsensical cajoler and consoler. His reasonableness enables him to understand that getting up in spring is worth the effort, that thinking up a story is just a matter of talking about what happens, that lost buttons can be found or replaced, that the way one looks in a swimming suit is not a matter of concern, and that letters can be sent and received if one has something to communicate. For every "ain't-it-awful" attitude that the distraught Toad projects, Frog provides a reasonable counterpoint. Together the amphibian friends embody two tendencies that exist in all of us. The story as a whole acts as a mediation between these two tendencies. The strong emotions of Toad are posed as problems that are solved with the help of the levelheadedness of Frog. This pattern is followed though multiple variations in the other books in the sequence—*Frog and Toad Together, Frog and Toad All Year,* and *Days with Frog and Toad.*

This basic device of the Frog and Toad books—the playing of an excessively emotional, overreacting clown against a calmly reasonable foil for humorous purposes—is not, of course, strictly the province of Lobel or the children's picture-book genre. A glance at other popular entertainments provides many examples. Pairs of comedians traditionally fall into this pattern. One plays the irrepressible silly, the other the dismayed "straight man." When we think of Abbott and Costello, Lewis and Martin, Lucille Ball and Desi Arnaz, Tom and Dicky Smothers, or any of the many other teams—we know instantly which one is the childlike goofy guy and which one is the seemingly adult tolerator of foolishness. To some extent, Lobel's success as a comic writer for kids (as well as the parents who also love his books) is the result of his discovery of a way to develop a kind of vaudeville in the context of attractively drawn picture books.

Another picture-book maker who has ingeniously adapted the comedy-team dynamic to the picture-book form is Bernard Wiseman, whose stories about Morris the Moose and Boris the Bear are absolutely hilarious. The goal of the Morris and Boris books is, however, entirely to produce belly laughs. Wiseman's books lack the lyrical and meditative qualities that give Lobel's books their underlying seriousness. Lobel makes his comedians hilarious while also enabling us to identify with them and feel genuine concern for their individual problems and their sometimes fragile relationship, despite the silliness of the situations. An important difference between Lobel's and Wiseman's comedy routines is that Lobel makes his fool less foolish and his straight man more calm and reasonable. In the Wiseman works, Boris is actually more emotional than Morris and spends much of his time exploding in angry frustration in ways that somewhat resemble Oliver Hardy's angry reactions to the pratfall blunders of Stan Laurel.

Now let's look at what happens when Lobel sends his straight man out on his own. As already indicated, the reasonable personality of Frog has much in common with the reasonable personality of the hero of *Grasshopper on the Road*. Grasshopper has the tall, slender body type of Frog, and he projects a calm and confident commonsensicalness. Because he is "on the road," Grasshopper's stories involve a varied cast of characters. Each of the eccentric insects he encounters on his way has an irrational obsession. These obsessions resemble those of Toad, but in the Grasshopper tales there is seldom any meeting of minds between the reasonable Grasshopper and the unreasonable creatures he meets. Grasshopper can find nothing to say to the beetles of the "morning club" that could stand any chance of persuading them that afternoons have their good points, too. Likewise, the fly who is obsessed with the absurd conviction that he must sweep clean the entire world, starting with the dirt road outside his door, will not listen to Grasshopper's advice. In the Frog and Toad books, Toad's absurd notions are part of the give and take of a relationship, but the silly notions of the insects Grasshopper meets are unredeemed by personality. Grasshopper merely needs to stay aloof and move on down the road. His life is not enriched by these eccentricities as Frog's is by Toad's. Here reasonableness has only to keep to its journey, turning aside from the misguided. The effect is largely satiric. We adopt Grasshopper's reasonable view as our own and find ourselves laughing at the human foibles that are exposed to ridicule through their depiction as the absurdly obsessive behaviors of the bugs Grasshopper meets along the way. The satiric perspective is so complete that we do not identify, even slightly, with the fools that the kindly, friendly Grasshopper must suffer gladly.

The unreasonable personality of Toad is given a different twist in *Owl at Home*. Lobel offered an interesting explanation of the difference between the two characters:

> Toad is a neurotic and Owl is psychotic. Toad is like most of us. He knows the limits. He never goes over the line. There's always a certain logic to everything he does. He's irritated because he's looking for something that he hasn't found. He's the kind of person who, if something goes wrong,

goes to bed. . . . But Owl is a complete psychotic. His grasp of reality is gone. In one chapter he tries very desperately to be in two places at once. . . . There's no sense of gravity to his thinking. It kind of completes the whole thing. (Natov and DeLuca, 90)

Owl "completes the whole thing" because he represents the foolishness of Toad taken to its logical extreme. Toad possesses a certain amount of "gravity" and is able to keep in touch with it through the reasonable interventions of Frog. It could be argued that Owl shows what could become of Toad without Frog.

Foolishness is extravagantly apparent in *Owl at Home*. Owl invites Winter to come inside to warm himself by the fire and then is dismayed at the havoc a door opened to winter weather wreaks on his home and his dinner. Strange bumps (his own feet) appear in Owl's bed at night and terrify the poor fellow with their unwillingness to go away. Owl's desire to be both upstairs and downstairs at once was mentioned by Lobel in the remarks quoted above. The oddest thing about *Owl at Home* is how remarkably likable Owl is and how easily we can put ourselves into his point of view. Lobel enables us to discover the impulsive fool inside ourselves. We recognize our own obsessions in his. A rather poetic further explanation for Owl's appeal might be offered. There is a mystical quality to Owl's relation to the world that seems justified by our underlying understanding that the universe is at some level an unresolvable mystery. Terrible and wonderful things happen to us and to others that we cannot explain to ourselves. Thus, while we can see through the silliness of Owl's conceptual mistakes, we share his feeling that "cozy" explanations *ought* to work. We, too, can see the appeal of having Winter or the Moon as a friend. We, too, would like there to be a mythos that would explain the universe and allow us to talk with it. We are amused by Owl's silliness, but we are also able to regard with pleasure a worldview that would make profundities into friendly neighbors.

The endings of the three kinds of books I discuss in this essay reveal the strategies toward personality that each kind of book develops. At the end of his book Grasshopper is "happy to be walking slowly down the road" (60) and secure in the knowledge that "the road would still be there in the morning taking him on and on to wherever he wanted to go" (62). The satisfaction that sustains Grasshopper is his self-reliance and the rewards of the successfully solitary journey. Owl's ending is just as solitary as Grasshopper's, but Owl does not have access to Grasshopper's realistic assessment of the reliability of the road and Grasshopper's knack for travel. Owl remains ever the divine fool, comfortably enrapt in the moonlight he has absurdly adopted as his buddy. As already suggested, Owl is sustained by the charmed life the author allows him. We accept Owl's successful solitude because that charmed life is, in fact, quite charming. Contrast these two solitary endings with the ending of *Frog and Toad All Year,* where the two radically different personalities treasure the satisfactions of friendship: "The two friends sat by the fire. The hands of the clock moved to show the hours of a merry Christmas Eve" (64).

Lobel's fictions explore the contrasting ways that the emotional and the reasonable may get on in their worlds. They may strike up a partnership that makes them into a kind of completed whole, or they may pursue their respective tendencies to see where they lead. A kind of faith that everything will somehow work out for the protagonists pervades all of these books. No dark night of the soul lies in wait in any of them, though there is an underlying sense that the choice of a manner of life is an important matter. We feel genuine sympathy for Toad when, in one of the tales in *Days with Frog and Toad,* Frog leaves a note saying he has gone off because he wants "to be alone" (52). We understand Toad's desperate worry that Frog may have decided not to be his friend any more. We can also understand that Frog's decision to go off to be by himself for a little while is a reasonable decision that contains no anti-Toad message. Frog's state of mind has much in common with the state of mind that enables Grasshopper to enjoy a life on his own out on the road. We can understand these personality-based preferences, and we recognize that they represent crucial choices. For all the genuine hilarity of Lobel's I Can Read books, they do also have "serious" value as demonstrations of how personality and personal choices operate in the world. These are valuable demonstrations for young children who are working on developing a sense of themselves as persons at the same time they are developing their ability to read, but, of course, they ring true for adults in the audience, too.

Although I Can Read books such as Lobel's were ostensibly designed in such a way that young readers could handle reading them independently, without parental intervention, in practice Lobel's books have proved extremely popular as read-aloud books, consumed over and over again by parent-child teams of readers. Lobel's knack for capturing the basic dynamics of human relationships and his deft sense of humor about how silly we all are have made his books ideal for read-aloud consumption. Parent and child are able to identify with and/or laugh at the adultlike Frog or the childlike Toad. The implicit wisdom of these humorous tales keeps parents aware that, although being a parent seems to require a Frog-like adult demeanor, nothing prevents parents from being rather Toad-like in their true selves. (Uncle Elephant's foolish, but quite competent, parenting gives this point a special twist.) Likewise, children are able, if they wish, to choose to think of themselves as the more adult personage or to delight in being the irrepressible, childlike clown—perhaps empowered by the perception that there is room in the world for both sorts of persons.

Perhaps the most surprising aspect of Lobel's display of basic possibilities is the implicit optimism the books convey about even the foolish protagonists. Frog and Toad provide balance for each other, and Grasshopper does not need any help, but how can we account for the silly Owl's confident persistence? Of course, Owl's success is unreasonable. He is a Don Quixote without the help of a Sancho Panza. Lobel's suggestion that an attractively silly soul can prosper seems an entirely personal gesture, and Lobel has said that *Owl at Home* is "one of the most personal books I've ever written" (Natov and DeLuca, 85). Owl's foolishness grows out of the context of his solitariness, and anyone who has spent a great deal of time alone can identify with the foolishness that rises to the top as the solitary Owl contemplates the mysteries of his little life. Lobel clearly feels that each of us is as capable of being foolish as we are of being reasonable. When asked whether he identified more with Frog or more with Toad, he replied that he believes "everybody is both" (73). He was quite capable of identifying entirely with the reasonable stance, as he does in his Grasshopper book and in most of his *Fables*, and yet he was also able to adopt the emotion-dominated state of mind of Toad or Owl and give voice to it with heartfelt sincerity. A quick sketch of Toad or Owl often accompanied his autographs of books at conferences, revealing, perhaps, the bond he felt with his more bewildered characters. Lobel's books taken as a whole embody for readers the truism that both the heart and the mind have their work to do.

WORKS CITED

Lobel, Arnold. *Days with Frog and Toad*. New York: Harper & Row, 1979.

———. *Fables*. New York: Harper & Row, 1980.

———. *Frog and Toad All Year*. New York: Harper & Row, 1976.

———. *Frog and Toad Are Friends*. New York: Harper & Row, 1970.

———. *Frog and Toad Together*. New York: Harper & Row, 1972.

———. *Giant John*. New York: Harper & Row, 1964.

———. *Grasshopper on the Road*. New York: Harper & Row, 1978.

———. *Owl at Home*. New York: Harper & Row, 1975.

———. *Uncle Elephant*. New York: Harper & Row, 1981.

Natov, Roni, and Geraldine DeLuca. "An Interview with Arnold Lobel." *The Lion and the Unicorn: A Critical Journal of Children's Literature* 1, No. 1 (1977): 72–97.

Wiseman, Bernard. *Morris and Boris*. New York: Dodd Mead, 1974.
———. *Morris Has a Cold*. New York: Dodd Mead, 1978.

OTHER WORKS OF INTEREST

Matthews, Gareth. "Literature for Children." *The Philosophy of Childhood*. Cambridge, MA: Harvard University Press, 1994. 104–7. (Published two years after my Lobel essay was written and published, Matthews' comments on *Frog and Toad Together* provide further corroboration, from a philosopher's point of view, of the simultaneously serious and comic appeal Lobel's works have for the dual audience of children and their parents.)

· 4 ·

The Cycle of the Seasons in
Hall and Cooney's *Ox-Cart Man*

Ox-Cart Man, written by Donald Hall and illustrated by Barbara Cooney, is one of those lucky instances of picture-book making where there is a felicitous compatibility between the text and the pictures. My purpose here is first to examine why the theme of the circularity of the seasons as presented in *Ox-Cart Man* is so powerfully appealing to Hall, Cooney, and their many readers; second to consider some of the ways both Hall and Cooney have separately explored somewhat different circular narratives; and third to suggest that works of art in which there is collaboration between poem and picture, particularly as handled in *Ox-Cart Man*, are ideally suited to the presentation of time as an endlessly repeating sequence.

To understand the nature of the appeal of *Ox-Cart Man* it is useful to note that it could be regarded as a remarkable reinvention of a form of word-image collaboration that was enormously popular during the Middle Ages. Books of hours, richly decorated prayer books, were "the best-selling books of the later middle ages, all over Europe, outselling any other text, religious or secular" (Collins and Davis, 31). Among the most popular features of a book of hours were their calendar sections that presented pictures of the labors or activities of the months. The most famous sequence of such images is the calendar pictures included in *Les Tres Riches Heures du Duc de Berry*, which were painted in the early fifteenth century primarily by the Limbourg brothers. The depictions of the months in aristocratically commissioned books of hours had clear-cut political dimensions. Part of the satisfaction the Duke of Berry would have taken in the seasonal illustrations of the Limbourg brothers has to do with pride and power of ownership. The depicted landscapes with their glorious chateaus belonged to the duke and his associates, and the depicted people were their subjects. These golden landscapes were cherished property preciously preserved for contemplation by the proprietor and his friends and relations. The medieval season sequence aims to capture the essence of twelve moments in time for the enjoyment of the powerful personage who, in a sense, owns everything the images reveal. The duke owns the people and the moment itself; the image eloquently stakes his claim.

The claim, however, is more than a worldly one. The season sequence establishes a timeless cyclical garden world in which the aristocrat who owns the garden could enjoy a kind of immortality. The form is fundamentally paradoxical. Attachment and detachment from the world are simultaneously expressed in the form: The particularities of the transient season are embraced and are understood to be transient, but the circular nature of the form essentializes the particulars so that they become eternal symbols of their moment, conceptualizations of a schema that is conceived of as infinitely repeating. The cycle of the seasons is the song by which the world sings itself. The form's circular nature implies that it is a song that will be endlessly performed. The garden of the duke, analogous as it is to the Garden of Eden, presents an implicit claim that the duke's reign is a timeless one. Such poetic dreams of sovereignty were, of course, often ruthlessly undercut by physical reality: The duke and the three Limbourg brothers all died in an epidemic before *Les Tres Riches Heures* could be completed. It was later finished by another artist for enjoyment by another patron.

I am not contending that *Ox-Cart Man* was deliberately concocted as an imitation of the medieval sequences of monthly genre scenes—its prototype, after all, was a poem by Donald Hall that was published before the children's picture-book collaboration with Barbara Cooney was undertaken; however, a number of resemblances between the popular modern book and its popular medieval forebears can be observed.

Ox-Cart Man begins with this statement:

> In October he backed his ox into his cart
> and he and his family filled it up
> with everything they made or grew all year long
> that was left over.

As the book continues the reader is given an illustrated catalog of the things the ox-cart man and his family produced during the various seasons of the year. Often we are told the month in which the item was produced. The emphasis on the labors of the months is obviously similar to the medieval depictions. Certain of the images—such as the shearing of sheep, the planting of seed, and the warming before a fire—have exact equivalents in the books of hours. Also, as in the books of hours, recognizable landscapes are presented as backdrops for the activities. Generally the depicted views seem to be generic New England landscapes and farm scenes rather than specific locales and architectures, but there is the impression in the scenes in the villages the ox-cart man passes through, and especially in the scenes in the town of Portsmouth, that we are seeing carefully researched re-creations of those long-lost built environments. Barbara Cooney is, in fact, well known for the careful attention that went into her images from the past. She visited the locales and searched out historical records (Smith and Schlangen, 188).

Hall and Cooney's book also shares with medieval works a cyclical view of the year. Although the reporting of the months in *Ox-Cart Man* is not handled as a straightforward calendar, we are clearly given to understand that all the tasks—the making of shingles, the bottling of maple syrup, the carving of brooms, the embroidering of linen, the making of candles, and so forth—will happen next year in much the same way they have happened in the year we have witnessed. The Limbourg brothers' vision of a world possessed by an aristocratic patron finds a kind of echo in *Ox-Cart Man*. The New England farmer seems fully in possession of his small domain. The self-sufficiency of the ox-cart man makes him almost as much the master of his tiny garden world as the Duke of Berry was of his. Furthermore, the ox-cart man's possession of his world and his mastery of the cycle of its seasons gives him command of the timeless realm captured in the images of the book. In experiencing either *Les Tres Riches Heures* or *Ox-Cart Man* we live a circle that does not seem to decline toward death and decay.

As we have seen, *Ox-Cart Man*, like season books of earlier times, fixes its narrative in a circular sequence that seems, in a limited but nonetheless tangible way, to defeat time and provide a taste of what it might be like to escape the falling action that culminates in the grave. It is important to note that the enduring appeal of both *Les Tres Riches Heures* and *Ox-Cart Man* is the result of the reader's identification with the proprietary protagonists. As we turn the pages, we imagine ourselves as the regal duke or the self-sufficient ox-cart man. We ride the cycle of the book's seasons and enjoy a taste of a circular eternity.

I would like now to glance briefly at other works by Hall and other works by Cooney to note the interest they have each separately shown in the presentation of circular time. Transcendence of death by wishful time travel is one of the central themes of Donald Hall's poetry. His poem "Ox Cart Man" (*Kicking the Leaves*, 47), upon which the picture book was based, is a rather subtle instance of his obsession with the possibility that time could be escaped through attending to the circularity of the seasons. Part of the power of this theme in both versions of the ox-cart lyric is that it is an understated implication of the work. Most readers of either version would say that the poem is an expression of fascination with the self-sufficiency of the New England farmer. The circular time of the piece provides satisfaction to the reader without making its presence initially obvious. In many other works by Hall we can observe, however, overt expressions of his interest in avoiding the passage of time as well as frank declarations of his fascination with turning back the clock. Much of his wishful time travel has to do with his affectionate regard for his grandfather Wesley Wells. Hall elegizes this esteemed elder in poem after poem and continually finds ways to imagine him alive and as he was when Hall was a child. For instance, in "Maple Syrup" (*Kicking the Leaves*, 25) an old jar of maple syrup left behind in the grandfather's cellar conjures him back to life. Innumerable other poems about his grandfather's house and grounds, where Hall has lived for a number of years, have similar small and large time-travel effects. Hall invokes similar magic in his bringing to life of his father, who died young. In a poem called "The Days" he parallels an exact moment and season in the present to its equivalent ten years in the past to rewind the tape of the decade:

> Ten years ago this minute, he possibly sat
> in the sunlight, in Connecticut, in an old chair:
> a car may have stopped in the street outside;
> he may have turned his head; his ear may have itched.
> Since it was September, he probably saw
> single leaves dropping from the maple tree.
>
> (*Old and New Poems*, 89)

The nonpassage of time also appeals to Hall in nonfamilial contexts, as testified to by his strangely wonderful poem about the nonarrival of Amelia Earhart, "Persistence of 1937," quoted here in its entirety:

> After fifty years Amelia Earhart's Lockheed fretted with rust
> still circles over the Pacific. From her skull's scrimshaw
> she peers downward, looking for a lane through permanent weather
> while a sixty-year-old man carves her story onto whalebone,
> slowly incising the fifth grader who paces from kitchen
> through living room to parlor back to kitchen, eating unbuttered
> slices of Wonder Bread, listening to the Philco for bulletins
> from the Navy: *After fifty years her Lockheed still circles.*
>
> (*Old and New Poems*, 213)

After the success of her pictures for *Ox-Cart Man*, which won the Caldecott Medal, Barbara Cooney's long, distinguished career as an illustrator took a turn toward a concentration more on works of her own author-ship and less on works where she served as an illustrator for another writer's words. Subsequent recent Cooney picture books were in a format and style that resembles her work for *Ox-Cart Man*. Likewise, these later works feature a manner of recollection of American ancestors that has much in common with the implicitly nostalgic attitude made famous by the popularity of *Ox-Cart Man*. There is a circularity to the plots of these beautiful books that no doubt derives, in part, from the example of *Ox-Cart Man*, but it is a circle that does not exclude death. In most of these books there is a child who grows to be an elder who tells his or her story to a child who is, in some sense, a descendent. The response of the descendent child to the example of the elder is to declare a desire to live a similar kind of life that will be carried out beyond the death of the elder. Thus the circle in this series of Cooney books is generational. There is no absolute denial of time and death, but there is a passing on of the torch of wisdom and understanding from one generation to the next, so that a kind of circular transcendence is achieved. Human existence is seen as an endless compound sentence: One clause is completed with a death, but there is always a conjunction that connects to another clause that is a child who begins it all again.

The best of these is *Miss Rumphius*, the first book of this type that Cooney did shortly after *Ox-Cart Man*. At the beginning of *Miss Rumphius* the protagonist—the small child, Alice Rumphius—receives the advice around which she will shape her life. Her beloved grandfather tells her the three secrets of the good life he has lived. To be like him, she must travel to faraway places, settle down when she is old in a house by the sea, and do something to make the world more beautiful. By the end of this charming book she has accomplished all three goals. The last and crucially important goal is realized when she spreads the seeds of lupine flowers far and wide. Also, by the end of the book Miss Rumphius's grand-niece, who has narrated the tale, runs off with an armful of lupines while declaring her intention to strive to achieve the same three goals, even though she has no idea how she will find her unique way to make the world more beautiful. The lovely circularity of the tale makes it seem a carefully shaped poetic performance, even though the narrative is presented in prose. A similar lyric circularity can be found in other Cooney books such as *Island Boy* and *Hattie and the Wild Waves*. Interestingly, in *Hattie*, which seems in some ways the most personal of Cooney's nostalgic books, the child lives up to a promise made to herself without the intervention of any direct influence by an elder. Although *Island Boy* has not won as much attention and as many awards as some of Cooney's other books, and its text is a trifle wordy, a case could be made that its pictures are the most beautiful Cooney was ever to make; its landscapes have a luminist sense of light and composition and atmospheric color that links Cooney's work to an important tradition in American art.

Cooney's work in the nostalgic picture-book form has created its own tradition. Her achievement in this area deserves to be better known. The horizontal design of *Ox-Cart Man*, which was Cooney's idea (Smith and Schlangen, 185), was ideally suited to a past-evoking narrative that involves a journey. In certain places in the story a panorama effectively characterizes the ox-cart man's trips to and from the Portsmouth market. Ideal for the evocation of antique worlds in miniature, this long, horizontal shape has been used with increasing effectiveness and variety in each of Cooney's subsequent, nostalgic books. As already indicated, *Island Boy* is a consummate demonstration of the possibilities of the form.

Imitators of Cooney have made considerable use of the horizontal composition for nostalgic tales that involve panoramas either to portray journeys or for some other reason. For instance, *Yonder*, with text by Tony Johnston and pictures by Lloyd Bloom, seems directly derivative from *Ox-Cart Man*, as does *The Olden Days* by Joe Mathieu. *The Glorious Flight Across the Channel with Louis Bleriot* by Alice and Martin Provenson, which won the Caldecott, shows to excellent advantage the strengths of the nostalgic-horizontal genre.

What even the best of the successors to *Ox-Cart Man* lacks, however, is the poetic text by Donald Hall, a text poetically rich and subtle in ways that can satisfy an adult fan of modern poetry, and yet, at the same time, compellingly simple enough to command the attention and enjoyment of a wide audience of children and adults, many members of which would not ordinarily seek out a free-verse modernist poem. Even Cooney's later works lack the subtle poetic features that Hall contributed to their ox-cart collaboration. Her subsequent nostalgic books have many excellences, but all must bear up under the weight of texts that are both more wordy and less lyric than *Ox-Cart Man*.

So quiet and fact preoccupied are Hall's well-chosen, though simple, words that most readers probably do not realize that they are reading a poem. But it is the attention to poetic nuance that gives the circularity of *Ox-Cart Man* its magical effect. The array of poetic devices—parallelism, the poetic catalog, the very short sentence, the very long sentence, and enjambment—that create these effects are easy enough to enumerate, though, of course, magic can never be entirely reduced to its devices. The model for the poem is primarily Whitman, who made all these devices—except the very short line—the signatory techniques of his most American of styles. It is also use-

ful to note that masterful use of the very short line was part of the legacy of
the other great American poetic innovator of the nineteenth century, Emily
Dickinson. Overtones of Whitman and Dickinson contribute to the historical feel of the text, but the primary reason for these devices is that they work
to make the poem Hall wants to make. Repetitive actions in a prosaic text
would have been boring, but Hall's use of parallelism makes those repetitions
beautiful and entertaining. Sentence after sentence begins with the statement
"He packed" as we are given the litany of the ox-cart man's tasks:

> He packed a bag of wool
> he sheared from the sheep in April.
>
> He packed a shawl his wife wove on a loom
> from yarn spun at the spinning wheel
> from sheep sheared in April.
>
> He packed five pairs of mittens
> his daughter knit
> from yarn spun at the spinning wheel
> from sheep sheared in April.
>
> He packed candles the family made.
> He packed linen made from flax they grew.

As the sentences proceed we find further patterns of parallelism. We note
that the preposition *from* tells us again and again where the packed items were
obtained. All the poetic devices can be seen to work in combination. The poetic catalog sometimes occurs as parallel phrasings concerning packing:

> He packed a barrel of apples
> honey and honeycombs
> turnips and cabbages
> a wooden box of maple sugar. . . .

Other times the poetic catalog is a parallel series of short sentences:

> He sold the bag of wool.
> He sold the shawl his wife made.
> He sold five pairs of mittens.
> He sold candles and shingles.
> He sold birch brooms.
> He sold potatoes.
> He sold apples.

Note, also, how the repetition of the words "He sold" continues the Whitmanesque parallelism of line and creates a balance between the two halves of the poem: The first part of the poem cataloged the packing of all the things that are later enumerated in their unpacking as goods for sale.

Enjambment is one of the results of several long sentences that stretch over several pages. It is perhaps awkward to use the word *enjambment*, since the book designers have probably not allowed Hall to entirely control his stanza formats, but, if we can apply the term loosely, we can see how the catalogs and the clause-after-clause long sentences reinforce the horizontalness of Cooney's format and pictures so that the reader seems, in some rather physical sense, to participate in the tasks and walk the journey through the manual labor of following the text and pictures from one page to the next. It is the rolling quality of the continuously linked poetic text that is key to what makes the circularity of *Ox-Cart Man* compelling. Hall and Cooney roll us along a path that passes the end of the journey and continues into the next year. We go past the return of the ox-cart man and find ourselves ending in a rather arbitrary but lovely way with the geese "dropping feathers as soft as clouds." Hall was able to underline the circularity of his poem more emphatically with the version of "Ox Cart Man" that appeared in *Kicking the Leaves* by concluding with the ox-cart man "building the cart again," but the loss of emphatic ending in the picture-book version of Hall's poem seems more than compensated for by the gain in verisimilitude and loveliness that results from slightly blurring the neatness of the circle.

Donald Hall's poem, likewise, becomes a more important and multifaceted work of art within the picture-book collaboration. The original poem is one of the high points of one of Hall's best collections of verse, but as the poetic text for what is destined to be an enduring classic of the picture-book form it achieves an unusual status in American popular culture. *Ox-Cart Man*, the picture book, is a more crucial and more richly satisfying work of art than the original poem, without necessarily being "better" in any literary way.

I would like to conclude, therefore, with the assertion that the compelling combination of picture and poem that is *Ox-Cart Man* makes possible a transcending circularity that neither Hall, who is not a painter, nor Cooney, who is not a poet, could achieve on their own. *Ox-Cart Man* is an illustrated poem worthy of admiration by adults who would not ordinarily be willing to admit to personally enjoying a children's book. Yet despite the genre-transcending beauty of what Hall and Cooney have achieved in *Ox-Cart Man*, the book remains, and has always been received as, a pleasant and unpretentious little picture book that any child could love and take to heart.

WORKS CITED

Collins, Marie, and Virginia Davis. *A Medieval Book of Seasons.* New York: Harper-Collins, 1992.

Cooney, Barbara. *Hattie and the Wild Waves.* New York: Viking, 1990.

———. *Island Boy.* New York: Viking, 1988.

———. *Miss Rumphius.* New York: Viking, 1982.

Hall, Donald. *Kicking the Leaves.* New York: Harper & Row, 1978.

———. *Old and New Poems.* New York: Ticknor & Fields, 1990.

———. *Ox-Cart Man.* Illus. Barbara Cooney. New York: Viking, 1979.

Johnston, Tony. *Yonder.* Illus. Lloyd Bloom. New York: Dial, 1988.

Longnon, Jean, ed. *The Tres Riches Heures of Jean, Duke of Berry.* Trans. Victoria Benedict. New York: Braziller, 1969.Mathieu, Joe. *The Olden Days.* New York: Random House, 1979.

Provensen, Alice, and Martin Provensen. *The Glorious Flight Across the Channel with Louis Bleriot.* New York: Viking, 1983.

Smith, Louisa, and Lisa Schlangen. "Integrity and Creativity: An Interview with Barbara Cooney." *The Lion and the Unicorn: A Critical Journal of Children's Literature* 16 (1992): 184–91.

The New York City
Picture Books of Maurice Sendak

$\mathcal{M}$y purpose here is to consider several Maurice Sendak books in which images inspired by New York City play an important part. I will be examining several different sorts of dream Manhattans, primarily in the picture books *In the Night Kitchen* and *We Are All in the Dumps with Jack and Guy*, but my discussion must be grounded in the realistic Brooklyn implicit in Sendak's illustrated stories for *The Sign on Rosie's Door*. My thesis is that there is in much of Sendak's best work an exciting tension between the mundane particularities of everyday life on the one hand and the theatrical glories of the fantasy life on the other. My emphasis on urban examples is, to some extent, an arbitrary limitation that will serve to keep this chapter to a reasonable length, but the limitation also aims to make possible an examination of Sendak's tendency to use the two faces of New York City—the Brooklyn of his childhood and the Manhattan of his childhood and his adulthood—as symbolic sites. As we shall see, although Sendak tends to equate Brooklyn with the mundane and Manhattan with the phantasmagoric, the two boroughs of his imagination are complexly interrelated, and the here-and-now particular and the far-away exotic are intermixed in every one of his urban pictorial narratives.

It comes as no surprise that discussions of *The Sign on Rosie's Door* have been dominated by Sendak's autobiographical commentaries on the year he spent recording, in notes and drawings, the antics and romanticisms of a "really" real Rosie, who lived across the street from his parents' Brooklyn home. Sendak has frequently spoken and written of Rosie as his primal character—the "ferocious," romantic, stubborn, courageous, and secretly vulnerable child from which all his child protagonists have derived. But Sendak's own Brooklyn childhood was also primary to the urban attitudes evident in Rosie and the many characters who followed after her; furthermore, in Rosie's yearnings for Broadway stardom we can see Sendak's own ferocious romanticism about the magicalness of Manhattan, that fabled place of lighted towers, food, and movie palaces.

The stories in *The Sign on Rosie's Door* demonstrate—in their deft, understated capturing of a theatrical yet needful child and of the energetic street life of children in one particular neighborhood—that Sendak is as much a writer as he is an artist. The unresolved nature of these stories is part of their gift of truth. To put it another way, although nothing terrible (or terribly important) happens in these stories, Rosie does have more than a little bit at stake. When the other kids go home, abandoning Rosie and breaking her hold on them so that our little star must sing "On the Sunny Side of the Street" to an empty backyard, Sendak lets us keep the sadness of it and does not resort to the sort of farcical resolution that concludes most of his picture books.

The stories in *The Sign on Rosie's Door* are told almost entirely through dialogue. The charm of the work derives from the amusing absurdity of what we hear the kids say in the midst of their make-believe play and from the seeming authenticity of each scene. Anyone who is still a child, or has overheard kids at play, or can reach back to memories of childhood, can recognize that Sendak has astutely observed and recorded persuasive enactments of childhood. Sendak's unpretentious achievement in his little collection of Rosie stories is a significant contribution to the "here-and-now tradition" in American children's literature.[1]

The here-and-now tradition has been well explained by Leonard Marcus in his biography of Margaret Wise Brown. The "fairy tale wars" is the term Marcus uses to describe a crucial rivalry and difference of opinion that worked itself out in the children's literature industry that developed and expanded from the 1920s through the 1940s. On the one side of the rivalry were the proponents of fairy-tale fantasy led by Anne Carroll Moore of the New York Public Library; on the other side were the advocates of the here-and-now storybook—stories based on the mundane experiences of everyday urban life, with an emphasis on capturing the kinds of things kids actually say—led by Lucy Sprague Mitchell, director of the Bank Street School. Margaret Wise Brown became the laureate for the here-and-now camp, but its later practitioners included such people as Ruth Krauss, many of whose works were fundamental exercises in getting the words straight from the mouths of children.[2]

Ruth Krauss was, of course, the here-and-now practitioner with whom Sendak had most contact. Sendak's work on *A Hole Is to Dig* and some of Krauss's other exercises in getting words straight from the mouths of children involved him in the here-and-now enterprise of constructing stories for kids by listening well. The here-and-now emphasis on urban life and on carefully observing and listening to children was clearly advantageous for Sendak. It gave him encouragement to find his stories on his Brooklyn street at a time when he was ready and able to engage in that sort of research. While colleagues of Sendak's, notably Ezra Jack Keats, built careers around the rich material of ordinary lives on city streets—Sendak's embrace of the unadorned urban moment was not sustained. Sendak had no desire to choose between fairy tales and urban scenes. The strategy of several of his best works has been to intermix the fairy-tale fantastic with the urban-moment mundane to create new and unusual works; of special importance in this regard are the exhilarating and magical *In the Night Kitchen* and the stern and nightmarish *We Are All in the Dumps with Jack and Guy*.

Kenny's Window—published four years before *The Sign on Rosie's Door* and sixteen years before *In the Night Kitchen*—clearly indicated both Sendak's obsession with fantasy and his interest in urban streets. The window through which Kenny dream travels to hobnob with a talking four-footed rooster, who lives in a vaguely defined magical garden, is a window in a realistically depicted Brooklyn brownstone, very similar to the ones Rosie and, of course, Sendak himself, lived in. In *Kenny's Window* the urban world of Kenny's street and Kenny's room predominate, at least visually, over Kenny's dream worlds. Even the Chagall-like visions of the flying rooster and the flying horse are suspended above the mundane urban architecture of Kenny's quite ordinary city street. The presentation of the fantastic within the context of the mundane that Sendak will so marvelously develop in *In the Night Kitchen* is implicit but largely unrealized in *Kenny's Window*. Though he wanted to envision subconscious dream material in this work—the book is dedicated, in part, to his analyst (Lanes, 64)—he is not quite ready to unlatch the window that he was to so gloriously throw open in his mature works.

The year after *Kenny's Window* appeared, Sendak published an illustrated book with a more parable-like plot about running away from home and then being happy to return that anticipates the plot of *Where the Wild Things Are* in certain respects, but, as in *Kenny's Window*, there is no departure from the mundane urban streets. *Very Far Away* turns out to be a bare room in an empty basement, where Martin and his animal friends necessarily need to manufacture their notions of the exotically far away inside their minds. The reader sees little glimpses of these fanciful realms in cartoon balloons above the characters' heads, but the artist does not give us any visual escape from the urban here and now of Martin's neighborhood. At the end Martin happily returns home to find contented resolution to his complaints.

The pictures in *Very Far Away* are more satisfying than those in *Kenny's Window*, but the biggest improvement is in the story. In fact, the story is a wonderful read-aloud piece that seems much more interesting without the pictures.[3] One striking and enjoyable discovery for attentive perusers of *Very Far Away* is the odd circumstance that the urban backdrop that appears to be Brooklyn on pages 17 through 21 suddenly changes to what appears to be Greenwich Village on page 23 through the end of the book. Perhaps Sendak was working on this volume when he made a move from his parents' home in Brooklyn to an apartment in Greenwich Village. Perhaps a book about running away from home struck a personal note concerning Sendak's desire for escape to the very far away known as Greenwich Village. This sort of little joke embedded in the details would be carried to extremes in his later books. Another amusing oddity in *Very Far Away* is a cameo appearance by Sendak himself, who rounds a corner walking his dog Jennie just as Martin emerges from the very-far-away basement.

Although a feeling for the details of modern urban life also lies at the heart of *In the Night Kitchen*, the here-and-now impulse is overwhelmed by a fairy-tale-like fantasy that is bizarrely inhabited by many of the essential ingredients of Sendak's urban childhood. Mundane details of a Brooklyn kitchen are everywhere, and everywhere they are shaped to resemble a caricature of the New York City skyline. A manic fantasy prevails. The tension between the ordinary, prosaic kitchen and the fabulous kingdom it has been made into are basic to the power of this tale. So intermingled are the beloved ordinary utensils and the dream-fantasy rendering of a Manhattan-evoking facade that it is not possible to separate one from the other. The real streets of Sendak's earlier books are no more to be seen. Dream has swallowed the urban world whole.

Sendak has commented in several places on how *In the Night Kitchen* grew out of his delightful childhood memory of visits to Manhattan, his love of movies—especially Mickey Mouse cartoons and Busby Berkeley musicals of the 1930s—and the eating-out occasions central to Manhattan visits (*Caldecott & Co.*, 166–67, 174–76); but this fantasy picture poem was also heavily influenced by the fairy tales and nursery rhymes that Sendak had been extensively studying. The fictions and poems of the anonymous oral tradition we refer to as the works of Mother Goose are key influences on *In the Night Kitchen*. Sendak and others (Lanes, 173–75; Cech, 182–83) have discussed the echoes of Mother Goose rhymes in the alternating verse-prose dynamic of *In the Night Kitchen*, but an obvious and important oral-traditions influence has not been much noticed. Cech has spoken of Sendak's three bakers as parallel to gods of fate in certain myths (202–3), but a more mundane folkloric parallel can be found in the innumerable tales of witches and other gruesome figures who await the accidental arrival of children for cooking in their ovens. Such evil crones are often portrayed as laughing and jovial despite their evil ways, making them not all that different from the jolly Oliver Hardy threesome. In some respects these three bakers cavort around their bowl of batter in a manner suggestive of the three witches in *Macbeth*. Despite the fairy-tale situation, *In the Night Kitchen* does not follow a fairy-tale plot. No witch or chubby chef gets shoved into the oven in the conclusion of this tale. Instead, the narrative, such as it is, follows the whimsical seminonsense pattern of a nursery rhyme. This text is poetic from first to last—one of the several masterpieces of picture poetry that the children's picture-book genre has given us. But the lack of a fairy-tale plot should not cause us to overlook the fairy-tale situation.

One of the explanations Sendak has given for his harmlessly demonic bakers and for the baking motif in general is that it is his "vendetta" against the Sunshine Bakery, which used to advertise, during the years Sendak was a child, that they "bake while you sleep." Sendak reports that his younger self found this notion distressing. How could they be so cruel as to do all this wonderful baking while poor little Maurice was sleeping and missing all this exciting action (*Caldecott & Co.*, 174–75)?

One of the reasons that we should pay careful attention to this motivation is that there is another even more powerful vendetta nested within the multiple meanings of this work. Sendak's vendetta has as its antagonist Death itself, subtly associated with the demise Mickey effortlessly averts. Sendak injects an element of fatality into his mysterious night bakery by use of the folkloric motif of the evil baker who cooks kids in the oven. The wit of this motif adds a sardonic undertone and an edge of real danger to this dream adventure. It also should not be overlooked that by adding little mustaches to the Sunshine Bakery bakers Sendak not only made them into Oliver Hardy clones but has also fused the benignly sunshine-bright advertising-logo bakers with the nightmarish image of Adolf Hitler, whose chambers for the extermination of Jews made him an enactment in recent historical time of the oven-stoking–wicked-witch character. The Hitler connection is a subtle undertone that Sendak himself may not have had consciously in mind as he developed the image, but it is a key ingredient in the work. Sendak's parents were both Jews who emigrated from Poland. It is hardly surprising that the Holocaust can be implicated in Sendak's books. The Nazi death camps are mentioned by most commentators on the nightmarish bakery of *We Are All in the Dumps*, but it could be argued that they are more crucial to consider as an underlying motif of *In the Night Kitchen*.

The jolly brightness of *In the Night Kitchen* stands in stark contrast to the circumstances of Sendak's life at the time he was writing it. His mother had just passed away, his father was diagnosed with a terminal illness, and Sendak himself suffered a serious heart attack. In a letter, Sendak explained the strength of character his hero is required to possess: "Mickey has to care about himself in every possible way, because I think he's in the land of the dead, for the most part. His parents are not to be found to help him. So then, with his nerviness, his sensibility, and his basic mind, he makes himself an airplane . . . he does something to sustain himself during his very suspenseful, strange, mystifying experience" (Deitch, 1984). The bravado of Mickey—who climbs out of an oven, makes and flies a plane over the "milky way," then dives down to the bottom of a bottle as tall as a three-story building—is a heroic response to the grim fact of mortality. During this magical adventure Mickey achieves several baptismal rebirths. Not only does he escape an oven but reemerges after two submersions—one in the batter and the other in an excess of milk. Sendak—who as a child was often sickly and on at least one occasion was not expected to live through the night—has constructed an unwavering superchild to triumph over the night. In addition to creating a picture-book masterpiece, he addresses his fears of death—the ultimate thing that goes bump (and thump, dump, clump, lump) in the night—at a time when it must have seemed everyone around him was dying.

Despite the grim context in which Sendak was creating this picture book, it is quite possibly Sendak's most boisterous and cheerful book. Paradoxically the Manhattanesque dream kitchen is, despite the initial menace of the ovens and the (demon) bakers, a place where something of legendary wondrousness can be made. It is a place of positive production; the place where ferment leads to product. Sendak's night kitchen is the deep, dark, dangerous, hard-to-get-to place where imagination resides. The fusion of the urban and the folkloric lies at the heart of this work's odd magic. The mythos of Manhattan carries with it the double suggestion that the Big City is simultaneously a place that can kill and a place where great things can be cooked up.

How did Sendak manage to fold his ferocious folk tale into a joyously magic Manhattan dream world? Winsor McCay's *Little Nemo in Slumberland* comic strips (circa 1907) that Sendak discovered just before creating *In the Night Kitchen* helped him arrive at the method for this lovely urban madness (*Caldecott & Co.*, 77–85). It is clear that many images in Sendak's picture book are directly derived from McCay: Most often cited are the images of Nemo falling through dream space, of little Nemo flopped half out of bed (with the bed and Nemo parallel to the picture plane), and of an inexplicably gigantic Nemo climbing around a toy version of Manhattan. More important than the specific borrowing of imagery was the example of McCay's use of the child dreamer. McCay's straight-ahead and rapid presentation of absurd dream worlds was a liberating influence. McCay makes no apologies and offers no complex literary framing devices to explain how Nemo gets to his dream world; he offers no tornados in Kansas, no falls down rabbit holes, and so forth. The dreams just happen to Nemo and last until he falls out of them. Sendak uses this simple formula to its best advantage.

If I am correct in my contention that Sendak manages to include some rather horrific allusions between the lines of *In the Night Kitchen*, one might ask how he decently accomplishes such things in a picture book for children. This is, of course, the same question that has hovered around all three of the books in his so-called trilogy. Taking seriously Sendak's tying of the three books together as a package will distract this discussion briefly from its urban theme, but a richer view of Sendak's success in his urban masterpiece, *In the Night Kitchen*, can be had if we briefly examine how he incorporated profound and menacing symbolism into delightfully comic and entertaining forms in all three works of his trilogy. A quick look at the layerings of meanings in *Where the Wild Things Are* and *Outside Over There* can help us define the similar dynamic in *In the Night Kitchen*. A full discussion of the allegorical nature of Sendak's three most admired and most often debated original books can be found in Geraldine DeLuca's 1984 essay, but a few key points can be made here.

Where the Wild Things Are was the first and bore the brunt of public complaint, though it is the most mild mannered of the three. *Outside Over There* is perhaps the most severely ominous of the three with its kidnapping of a baby by demonic goblins represented as shadowy hooded figures that seem to have been modeled after the murderous dwarf of the movie *Don't Look Now*—a horror film, based on a Daphne Du Maurier story, that came out in the mid-1970s around the time Sendak would have been at work on *Outside Over There*. The standard answer—along the lines that Sendak helps children of all ages face their fears—begs the question. The strategy Sendak uses to sail past the anxiety of most readers derives from his clear grasp of the basic dynamic of the cartoon tale. The example of the steady march through absurdity presented in Winsor McCay cartoons is not Sendak's only source for his use of a self-confident protagonist and a plot that is stylized farce. At the heart of these three Sendak masterworks is the movie cartoon as given distinctive form by Disney and developed further by others. Mickey Mouse is one prototype of the unflappable protagonist; Warner Brothers' Bugs Bunny is another. Max is in no more danger from the silly wild things than Bugs Bunny is from the gun-wielding Elmer Fudd.[4] Each of the three trilogy protagonists faces challenges, and the challenges become more and more formidable as the trilogy develops. Max's wild things only look dangerous. They are pushovers from the first moment of Max's resistance. Mickey, however, seems lost to us for a short time; he is entirely submerged in batter and thrust into the oven before he pokes through and begins to take charge of the situation. The urban demeanor of the night kitchen, while in many respects jazzy and fun, does not offer easy comfort to the heroic Mickey. Mickey's stalwart heroism is, in fact, underscored by his situation as a child alone in the city night. The third work in the trilogy, *Outside Over There*, goes beyond the influence of the simple cartoon farce[5] and shows the influence of Disney epics such as *Pinocchio*, which was Sendak's favorite animated Disney film (*Caldecott & Co.*, 111–17). Comic antics do not carry either Ida or Pinocchio easily past their difficulties. In these two stories the protagonists fail rather completely before they finally rise to the occasion and triumph.

In addition to the masterful use of cartoon farce, Sendak adds delight and verve to his rendering of the dark adventures presented in his trilogy by the deft use of poetic form. A substantial commentary on Sendak's use of verse in his trilogy is available in Amy Sonheim's book. She comments on how Sendak uses formal verse to decorate and enliven the dark and dangerous moments in these books. For instance, the ordinary world of Mickey's going to sleep is narrated fairly prosaically, but the world of the dream bakers is charged with poetic intensity (105–10). The pattern here can be likened to the situation at the beginning of *Macbeth*, where the intensely poetic chantings of the three witches contrast sharply with the blank-verse conversation of Macbeth and Banquo. Both the farcical nature of the cartoon catastrophes and the formality of poetic language serve to bounce the protagonists blithely through the dark nights of Sendak's soul in his three big books.

Sendak's use of visual and verbal liveliness to delight and animate the work creates situations where it might be possible to be frightened the first time through any of these three books, but where most readers will find the works a happy romp in subsequent rereadings. As works of poetry, these books are intended primarily for rereading. (The first reading is simply a necessary warm-up procedure.) Any adult who has endlessly reread *Where the Wild Things Are* to a child can confirm the magicalness of the work's poetic effects.

The versions of New York City implicit in *The Sign on Rosie's Door* and *In the Night Kitchen* are largely artifacts of Sendak's childhood—a carefully observed Brooklyn on the one hand and a dream Manhattan on the other. *We Are All in the Dumps with Jack and Guy* gives us nightmare renderings of both Brooklyn and Manhattan, but the dream world presented this time does not seem as thoroughly dreamed as the magic amalgam of Manhattan skyline and Brooklyn kitchen Sendak gives us in *In the Night Kitchen*. Despite its origin as the visualization of two almost nonsensical nursery rhymes, *We Are All in the Dumps* seems rather calculating and over full of visual explanation. While making slides of the book, I became exasperatingly aware of how redundant the pictures are. In several cases similar images follow one after the other to impose a prosaic and somewhat bulky storyline on the frail frame of the lovely, strange little Mother Goose rhymes. *In the Night Kitchen* is a masterful picture poem whose hard-earned and pain-inspired lyricism carries us through a deeply felt reverie full of laughter and delight, but *We Are All in the Dumps* is a heavy-handed moral lecture that seems to come more from Sendak's head than from his heart.

The case in favor of admiring *We Are All in the Dumps* has, however, been well argued by Peter Neumeyer, who notices much of interest in this richly allusive and handsome book. Neumeyer catalogs the allusions to Blake's chimney sweeps, the fleeting fly-by appearance of Mozart as an angel, the sad demise of picture-book maker James Marshall, the photographs of street urchins by Jacob Riis, the AIDS epidemic, the starving children of an African drought, the note of thanks to Iona Opie for her help with the nursery rhymes, and multiple other little reflections, jibes, and jokes. Perhaps Neumeyer's most interesting identification of allusions is the religious images—a deposition, a pieta, and a resurrection that are presented as the "Poor Little Kid" transcends his near-demise. Neumeyer makes much of the beauty of the double-page spread in which the kid is taken down from the moon (in a deposition-like way).[6]

In *We Are All in the Dumps* Sendak gives us an image of a city of the 1990s in which the homeless huddle together inside cardboard boxes, which also suggests in fascinating ways the impoverished London of Charles Dickens or of William Blake. Although this fable cobbles together several times and places, we are located primarily in New York City, but there is no love of the Big Apple evident in this book. Sendak gives us here neither a marvelous Manhattan nor a beloved Brooklyn. Cameo appearances by Trump Tower and the Brooklyn Bridge do, however, confirm those habitats as the contexts for these mean streets.[7]

It is instructive to contrast the apathetic shaven-headed waifs of *We Are All in the Dumps* with the prancing, full-of-fun, mischievous kids we witnessed in *The Sign on Rosie's Door*. Both sets of youngsters are seen in streets, but in the two cases the circumstances and attitudes of the children are very different. Rosie and friends are out in the street to play, and for Rosie all her play points toward future glory—her impossible but lovely dreams of some-day being a Broadway star. By contrast, Jack and Guy and company just want to survive and keep the rats at bay. The "poor little kid" is a dreamless victim.

Obviously there are allusions to the Holocaust implicit in the orphan-age and bakery to which the kittens and the poor little kid are taken by the villainous rats; however, the unexplained escape of the kid to the field of rye where Jack and Guy find him, as Sendak strains to shape his tale to the words of the nursery rhyme, seems, to me at least, to deflate the threat of this sup-posed Holocaust. There is no coherence to the kidnapping and no plausibil-ity to the escape of the sickly child. The storage of the kittens on shelves could be suggestive of the way Jews were treated in the death camps, but it is not entirely clear how that allusion is supposed to work. For anyone who has dealt with kittens or children such open-shelved storage has scant plau-sibility. Why would a kitten stay on a shelf? No wonder the kid got away if this is the way the rats confine their prisoners. Sendak has often praised Ran-dolph Caldecott's illustrations of nursery rhymes, and this book must be, in part, an effort to equal that master. But Caldecott's illustrations, as odd as they sometimes are, never lack inherent plausibility. Sendak's fantasy here tries so hard to accommodate all the details of both nursery rhymes that he does not entirely succeed in keeping his plot under control.

The greatest peculiarity of this book, and the vehicle for Sendak's ser-monizing, is the annoying, know-it-all moon he shoves into our faces. One of the most repetitive elements in the book visually, this celestial busybody is somewhat of an insult to the reader's intelligence. It is there in frame after frame dictating how we should react to each scene. This inescapable know-it-all is a representation of a stern adult conscience and seems the comple-mentary opposite of the rebellious child that is the dominant figure in most of Sendak's best books. The moon's looking over the shoulder of the char-acters and its intervention as a deus ex machina to save the day and force Jack and Guy to participate in the rescue makes the supposed protagonists almost unnecessary.

This moon is, however, central to some gorgeous picture making. There is, for instance, considerable visual excitement to the moon's entry into the action. It is wonderful to see this fabulous globe-with-a-face pick up Jack and Guy in its mouth and transport them to the site of rescue, and there is magic to the moon's leap into the fray in the form of a gigantic cat (with a fascinating Cheshire-cat grin). But for all its graphic interest, the moon-cat's pomposity makes it a narrative liability.

The moon as observer of kids in the street constitutes a kind of return to the observation of kids Sendak gave us in *The Sign on Rosie's Door*, but the observer of Rosie and her friends was Sendak himself, a largely invisible presence watching only to appreciate and never to judge. Sendak's creation of the harshly judgmental moon observer indicates a shift in attitude and sympathies of which Sendak himself may not be aware. Perhaps he no longer finds it easy to identify with children. (He has, perhaps, sent his "inner child" to its room.) Sendak's championing of the impoverished, the ill, and the abandoned is admirable, but the use of his remarkable talents to scold and to admonish seems less than its best use.[8]

Though the hectoring moral tone of Sendak's images for *We Are All in the Dumps* makes it less than his most delightful work, there is an operatic magnificence to this production—the result, perhaps, of Sendak's extensive theatrical work in recent years—that makes it a fascinating return by Sendak to the picture-book enactment of the urban here-and-now. In the here-and-now of the urban 1990s, Rosie and her Brooklyn pals are starving and apathetic, there is no chicken soup with rice in sight, and the Manhattan dream world has become entirely nightmare.

No doubt the shift in Sendak's attitude toward Manhattan that takes place in the interim between *In the Night Kitchen* and *We Are All in the Dumps* is, at least in part, reflective of Sendak's personal shift of feelings toward life in the Big City. The romance of Manhattan's bright glitter and relentless energy seems to have become less satisfying for him for a variety of reasons. Not long after the publication of *In the Night Kitchen* Sendak moved his primary residence to rural Connecticut for reasons of "health" and "solitude." Sendak's darker view of Manhattan in *We Are All in the Dumps* and his illustration work for a new edition of Herman Melville's *Pierre, or the Ambiguities* would seem to reflect a willingness on Sendak's part to acknowledge that Manhattan can be seen to have much in common with the dismal London of Blake or Dickens. That the magical Manhattan has not entirely receded for Sendak can be observed in his hilarious illustrations for Arthur Yorinks's *Miami Giant*, which enacts a delightfully silly revision of the King Kong story. But it is worth noting that the giants' bad experiences in Manhattan cause them to flee back to Miami. The closest they are said to come to a return to Broadway is a rumored move to suburban Long Island.

Sendak's illustrations for Melville's *Pierre, or the Ambiguities*—a brutally adult book for which Sendak's illustrations envision a cruel and claustrophobic nineteenth-century New York City—could be seen as the climactic descent of Sendak's bold, rebellious child into the despairs of darkest adulthood. In a review of Sendak's illustrations for Melville's *Pierre*, Jed Perl notes that

> Our memories of all Sendak's slyly exultant heroes and heroines are buried deep inside Pierre's wild-eyed, incredulous look in the book's last, awful illustration. . . . The kid has grown up and lost, and Sendak is right there by his side. (34)

It is, however, hard to believe that Sendak's rebellious child will accept permanent defeat. As Mickey rose again from the bread dough, as Max stared down all monsters, and as Ida rescued her sister from the goblins, so can we expect the indomitable Sendak child to recover his or her audacity in future books. It will be interesting to see if the next phase in Sendak's work will emphasize his interest in the dark woods of the fairy tale that has been steadily increasing in his mature work or if his continuing preoccupation with urban scenes will be carried further or if he will find new ways to merge his dangerous places. It seems unlikely, however, that Sendak will ever return to the understated treatment of here-and-now lives of children on ordinary city streets. His mature works are all too grandly operatic to allow room for a lovely little one-note singer like Rosie.

NOTES

1. Lucy Sprague Mitchell's 1921 collection entitled *Here and Now Story Book* surprises readers by beginning with a long, polemical introduction by Mitchell, "What Language Means to Young Children," which she pointedly addresses "to parents, teachers and writers." Although Mitchell did not insist that a here-and-now tale had to be urban in focus, Mitchell and her Bank Street colleagues were very attentive to the fact that the here and now for their students was New York City. Furthermore, the predominantly city-oriented nature of the tales in *Here and Now Story Book* suggests that Mitchell regarded the city as the inevitable environment for most modern children. This assumption pervades much material for children that grew out of the progressive education movement. Some of the preoccupations of the *Sesame Street* television series, for instance, could be regarded as direct descendents of Mitchell's *Here and Now Story Book*.

2. Sendak greatly admired Margaret Wise Brown and included an essay in tribute to one of her books in his *Caldecott & Company* (125–27) collection of essays and interviews. Among the many Brown-derived motifs that can be observed in Sendak's work are his use of sounds in ways that recall Brown's here-and-now "noisy books" (the "racket" Mickey hears coming from the night kitchen is an obvious instance)

and his deployment of the moon in ways that recall *Goodnight Moon* and other moon-obsessed Brown books.

3. Because *Very Far Away* is more interesting as a literary piece than as an example of Sendak's visual art, listening to it as presented by Tammy Grimes on her audio recording of Sendak's work reveals the strength of the piece more clearly than an examination of the book itself. Sendak's deft and suggestive text enables the reader to conjure visions of "very far away" that the pictures, drawn in the understated style he often employed in the 1950s, cannot equal.

4. It should be noted that Charlie Chaplin was a big influence on the cartoons that influenced Sendak, and, of course, Sendak was also directly influenced by the farcical antics and transcendent grace of Chaplin's best sequences.

5. Many sorts of aesthetically diverse influences enriched and deepened the composition of *Outside Over There*. For example, there were Sendak's continuing studies of the tales of the Brothers Grimm with their dark plots concerning evils done or threatened. Also, Sendak and others have commented on his preoccupation with Mozart—including the fantastical opera *The Magic Flute*—during the time he was creating *Outside Over There*. Furthermore, Michael Steig has proposed, and Sendak has confirmed, the influence of George MacDonald's *The Princess and the Goblin* on *Outside Over There*. The tapestries of influence discoverable in Sendak's mature works are evidence of his openness to inspiration and his knack for articulating his admirations of older materials in the form of eccentrically original new picture books.

6. There is an interesting similarity between Sendak's deposition image and a scene of similar loveliness in Tomie dePaola's *Sing, Pierrot, Sing*. Sendak probably borrowed the image directly from Renaissance art, but the scene in dePaola's book might have alerted him to the possibility.

7. Peter Neumeyer misidentifies the bridge as the Queensborough Bridge (34), most likely because he is assuming that the derelict part of the city in the foreground would be Queens, but it is important to my discussion to understand that Sendak has included the Brooklyn Bridge, a symbol of his ongoing concern with Brooklyn, the borough of his childhood days.

8. Another example of Sendak's impulse toward the didactic adult point of view can be found in a book he published in 1976 called *Some Swell Pup*, which is an extended lecture on the proper treatment of pets. In this pompous book a hooded dog figure acts as an intervening know-it-all in a manner that resembles the behavior of the bossy moon of *We Are All in the Dumps*. Although it could be pointed out that "cautionary tales" can be found at every phase of Sendak's career, a look at Sendak's best-known early cautionary tale, *Pierre* of the Nutshell Library boxed set of small volumes, reveals that, although Pierre does eventually curb his cantankerousness enough to admit the value of "caring," the emphasis in the story as a whole is on Pierre's insistent preference for preferring not to care. For the most part the emphasis in most of Sendak's early works, even when they are cautionary tales, is predominantly on the stubborn, rebellious energy of the child. Sendak's parable of the boy who allowed himself to be eaten by a lion because he "did not care" is returned to

us in a new way with *We Are All in the Dumps*, which ferociously insists upon compassion, but this time the ferocity is the province of the adult perspective. (The phrase "prefer not to" is an allusion to Melville's *Bartleby*, which Sendak also has in mind.)

WORKS CITED

Cech, John. *Angels and Wild Things: The Archetypal Poetics of Maurice Sendak*. University Park: Pennsylvania State University Press, 1995.

Commire, Anne, ed. "Sendak, Maurice," *Something About the Author*, Vol. 27. Detroit: Gale, 1982.

Deitch, Gene. Audio letter, April 19, 1984. Weston Woods Studios production archives, quoted by Cech (202).

DeLuca, Geraldine. "Exploring the Levels of Childhood: The Allegorical Sensibility of Maurice Sendak." *Children's Literature* 12 (1984): 3–24.

Grimes, Tammy. *Where the Wild Things Are, In the Night Kitchen, Outside Over There and Other Stories by Maurice Sendak*. Performed by Tammy Grimes (audio cassette). New York: Caedmon, 1988.

Krauss, Margaret. *A Hole Is to Dig: A First Book of First Definitions*. New York: Harper-Collins, 1952.

Lanes, Selma. *The Art of Maurice Sendak*. New York: Abrams, 1980.

Marcus, Leonard. *Margaret Wise Brown: Awakened by the Moon*. Boston: Beacon, 1992.

McCay, Winsor. *Little Nemo in the Palace of Ice and Further Adventures*. New York: Dover, 1976.

Melville, Herman. *Pierre, or the Ambiguities*. Ed. Hershel Parker. Illus. Maurice Sendak. New York: HarperCollins, 1995.

Mitchell, Lucy Sprague. *Here and Now Story Book*. New York: Dutton, [c.1921] 1948.

Neumeyer, Peter. "We Are All in the Dumps with Jack and Guy: Two Nursery Rhymes with Pictures by Maurice Sendak," *Children's Literature in Education* 25, No. 1 (1994): 29–34.

Perl, Jed. "Where the Wild Things Are." *The New Republic*, March 18, 1996. 30–34.

Sendak, Maurice. *Caldecott & Co.: Notes on Books and Pictures*. New York: Farrar, Straus and Giroux, 1988.

———. *Hector Protector and As I Went Over the Water*. New York: Harper & Row, 1965.

———. *In the Night Kitchen*. New York: Harper & Row, 1970.

———. *Kenny's Window*. New York: Harper, 1956.

———. *Nutshell Library*. New York: Harper & Row, 1962.

———. *Outside Over There*. New York: Harper & Row, 1981.

———. *Really Rosie*. Music: Carole King. New York: HarperCollins, 1975.

———. *The Sign on Rosie's Door*. New York: HarperCollins, 1960.

———. *Some Swell Pup, or Are You Sure You Want a Pup?* Written with Matthew Margolis. New York: Farrar, Straus & Giroux, 1976.

————. "Sources of Inspiration," *The Zena Sutherland Lectures, 1983–1992*. Ed. Betsy Hearne. New York: Houghton Mifflin, 1993. 1–25.

————. *Very Far Away*. New York: Harper, 1957.

————. *We Are All in the Dumps with Jack and Guy*. New York: HarperCollins, 1993.

————. *Where the Wild Things Are*. New York: Harper & Row, 1963.

Sonheim, Amy. *Maurice Sendak*. New York: Twayne Publishers, 1991.

Yorinks, Arthur. *The Miami Giant*. Illus. Maurice Sendak. New York: HarperCollins, 1995.

OTHER WORKS OF INTEREST

Brown, Margaret Wise. *The Noisy Book*. Illus. Leonard Weisgard. New York: Harper-Collins, 1939.

Cott, Jonathan. "Maurice Sendak: King of All Wild Things." *Forever Young*. New York: Random House, 1977. 187–219.

Grimm, Wilhelm. *Dear Mili*. Trans. Ralph Manheim. Illus. Maurice Sendak. New York: Farrar, Straus & Giroux, 1988.

Grimm, Wilhelm, and Jacob Grimm. *The Juniper Tree and Other Tales from Grimm*. Trans. Lore Segal and Randall Jarrell. Illus. Maurice Sendak. New York: Farrar, Strauss & Giroux, 1973.

————. *King Grisly-Beard*. Trans. Edgar Taylor. Illus. Maurice Sendak. New York: Farrar, Straus & Giroux, 1973.

Keats, Ezra Jack. Various picture books, including *Snowy Day* and *Whistle for Willie*.

Nodelman, Perry. *Words about Pictures: The Narrative Art of Children's Picture Books*. Athens: University of Georgia Press, 1988.

Opie, Iona, and Peter Opie, eds. *The Oxford Dictionary of Nursery Rhymes*. Oxford: Clarendon Press, 1951.

Schwarcz, Joseph H., and Chava Schwarcz. "Sendak's Trilogy: A Concept of Childhood," *The Picture Book Comes of Age*. Chicago: American Library Association, 1991. 194–205.

Sendak, Maurice. *Higglety Pigglety Pop! or There Must Be More to Life*. New York: Harper & Row, 1965.

————. *Seven Little Monsters*. New York: Harper & Row, 1976.

Sipe, Lawrence. "The Private and Public Worlds of *We Are All in the Dumps with Jack and Guy*." *Children's Literature in Education* 27, No. 2 (1996): 87–108.

Steig, Michael. "Coming to Terms with *Outside Over There*." *Stories of Reading: Subjectivity and Literary Understanding*. Baltimore: Johns Hopkins University Press, 1989. 202–20.

Zornado, Joseph L. "Maurice Sendak and the Detachment Child." *Inventing the Child: Culture, Ideology and the Story of Childhood*. New York: Garland, 2001.

· 6 ·

Dashing Heroes and Eccentric Families in William Joyce's Picture Sagas of Our Common Culture

*W*illiam Joyce's meticulously beautiful picture books have multifarious popular-culture dimensions that are central to their vitality and their appeal to a broad audience of children and adults. Joyce has explained that his books "hearken back to the sort of shared popular culture that we all grew up with on television—Flash Gordon from the thirties, the Stooges from the forties, Bugs Bunny from the fifties. Growing up watching television, you would see this constant barrage of cool stuff. . . . It's become a sort of shared sensibility" (Telgren, 134). Joyce's achievement turns inside out the dire warnings that began in the 1950s and continue to this day. Joyce apparently spent a goodly portion of his 1960s childhood watching television, and, far from rotting his brain, this "vast wasteland" fueled his extraordinary picture-book-making imagination. As this chapter proceeds I will argue that the shared sensibility he refers to contains (in addition to television shows) classic picture books, series books, comic books, advertising art, toys, fashions, auto styles, and famous works of fine art. Television of the 1960s offered the young Joyce a compendium of inspirations; it seems to have served him as an easily available museum of popular culture.

Joyce's artistic means to the capturing of this shared sensibility is not, however, entirely popular in its approach. The striking beauty of Joyce's work—his knack for rising above the visual mediocrity of much popular culture work—has much to do with his incorporation of fine-arts influences and his overriding tendency toward elegant refinement of technique. Fine-arts elements are much more important than Joyce ever admits to in his statements about his illustrations. His borrowings from the fine arts (as well as from popular works heavily influenced by the fine arts) are often what give his designs their compositional power. Meanwhile, his borrowings from the more disposable of the popular arts often supply much of his antic wit. At all times it is difficult to sort his overlapping antecedents. As he puts it, his ideas are "all smushed up inside [his] head" (*Scrapbook*, 6). Ultimately, a definitive separating out of Joyce's influences is less important than grasping the joyousness that underlies his constructions. The vigorous delights of Joyce's illustrated world emerge as fortuitously playful gestures. While keeping his adult sophistication in charge of his technique, Joyce lets his inner child control his imagination. The "common culture" he wants us all to share has much to do with the sensibility he discovered for himself as a child. Joyce's embrace of the extravagant silliness of popular culture is crucial to the celebration of shared culture and sensibility that his work develops. His generous embrace of the popular provides him with a rich array of images and stylistic features without blocking him from giving his work sophistications of design derived from his training in artistic and cinematic modes. While Joyce rejoices in his role as the whimsical scribe and high priest for a shared nostalgic sensibility, his distillations both depend upon and transcend the cultural elements he celebrates. His training as a fine artist and a filmmaker equip him with the means to create works that are often more beautiful and artistically interesting than the "cool stuff" that inspired them.

Joyce's strong grasp of principles of cinematic design was accentuated during his college days at Southern Methodist University when he switched his major from the studio art program to the filmmaking program. Images from the silver screen, which first became important to Joyce during his television-obsessed childhood, have provided him with models for the melding of the popular and vigorously vulgar with the solidly crafted. Joyce understood that powerful visual composition in film contributed to the success, both artistic and financial, of both low-brow and high-brow classic films.

The strong compositions of still photos and painted posters used to promote movies seem also to have influenced Joyce both directly and through the intermediary of comic books, which were themselves influenced by movie posters. Such influences are multiply dynamic, as film posters and stills were themselves influenced by comic books and pulp-novel illustrations—especially the sort used on covers. The circularity of such patterns of influence makes them untidy and difficult to assess.

In this discussion I focus on works for which Joyce produced both images and words. I examine the mix of popular and fine-arts elements that are reflected in each work, but the organization of my survey of the Joycean world stresses two major themes that have been prominent in all books of his published thus far. It is my contention that each of his self-authored picture books is organized around either the celebration of an eccentric family or the exposition of a tale of heroic action. The heroic actions are usually of a swashbuckling, cinematic sort. There is much overlap and interweaving of these two types of stories in the works discussed here: His eccentric family sagas always contain some elements of heroic endeavor, and his heroic adventures always have familial contexts or consequences.

For each work I discuss I mention several of the major influences or echoes evident in the work. Because Joyce's pictures have influences that range from the grandest of Renaissance art to the most modest of comic strips, it is not easy to do justice to his antecedents. I endeavor, however, to give some sense of the "common culture" presented in his works.

HEROIC SAGAS

My examples of heroic sagas are *George Shrinks, Bentley & Egg, Santa Calls,* and *The Leaf Men and the Brave Good Bugs.*

George Shrinks (1985)

Joyce's first heroic adventure tale was also his first self-authored picture book. Crucial to the excitement of *George Shrinks* is the boldly active and strikingly confident nature of George's attack upon the tasks he performs despite the bizarre disadvantage of his reduced state. George's confidence and bravado bring to mind the heroic behaviors of silver-screen swashbucklers of the sort portrayed by such actors as Errol Flynn, but there is also a suggestion of the boyish straight-ahead-ness of the heroes of boy novels from Tom Sawyer through Tom Swift.

Although many commentators routinely assume that George is asleep and dreaming his adventures as a three-inch-high boy (Cech, 19), the text and pictures do not unambiguously support that view. In fact, a case can be made, using evidence from the pictures, that he has been subject to a magical transformation in the "real" world rather than a sleep-induced dream fantasy.[1] Readers do not need to resolve this question. No doubt Joyce wanted to leave the "reality" of the adventure unresolved. It seems likely that Joyce would lean toward the "reality" interpretation, because to say an adventure is "just a dream" is to lessen its potency. As we shall see in his other works, Joyce clearly favors the empowerment of the fantastic.

Ultimately, it does not matter whether George is supposed to be literally asleep. The principle that controls his fantastic shrunken adventures is more cinematic than it is dreaming (of the nocturnal sort). Joyce's training as a filmmaker seems often to come to the fore as he conceptualizes his illustrations. He has commented that "when I am working on a book, it plays as a movie in my head" (Telgen, 133). This filmic progression is especially clear in *George Shrinks* where one image often anticipates and moves toward the next in ways that are suggestive of a storyboard for a film shoot. The most structurally cinematic parts are the bed scenes at the beginning and the end and the airplane scene that starts just past the middle of the book and carries on almost to the end.

As we move through the early to middle parts of the book, we are given one-page-per-adventure accounts of George's strange and wonderful exploits. Some scenes are hilarious, single-image tales that operate almost as film stills (which are complete narratives in the way history paintings are complete narratives), but even the largely self-contained scenes are played toward or against the image developed in its facing page. Double-page spreads always suggest a pairing of some sort and a flow of action from left to right.

The first bed sequence has a full-sized George hugging his stuffed bear as the book begins. The next image in the sequence, showing a tiny George still asleep by his bear, was used as the frontispiece for the book and is, thus, out of sequence. The second captioned image offers a view down the pillow that shows George's waking to confront his reduced state, emphasized by the sudden hugeness of the toy bear, and provides a full view of the note from his parents, a towering paper tent toward which he is gazing. George then turns to face the vast landscape of his bedroom with a stance that expresses surprise and readiness for movement. His engaged posture suggests a heroic explorer facing a formidable landscape, which is really just a low-angle view of his bed and the doors of his closet and room. There is a sense that the "camera" has turned toward the direction he will need to move. The "camera" shifts again, and we see George and his bed in profile so that we can watch George pull up his blanket to begin his heroic fulfillment of his parents' instructions, starting with "please make your bed." The ongoing carrying out of the parental directives provides the text and primary plot of the book.

In the next frame George has left the bed behind as he gazes around the corner at his principal antagonist, his cat. We realize that George has ventured down from the relative safety of his bedtop to the edge of his room. This is the only image in the first half of the book that has no caption. It underscores the potential menace of the cat that will become an important part of the purely visual heroic plot, which operates parallel to the parental-note-driven plot.

A strong pairing of actions occurs in the next double-page spread where George sits on a bathtub faucet and brushes his teeth with a comically huge brush, followed by an image of George at sea in the tub firing his toy-boat cannon at his rubber ducky. George brushing with a brush twice his size is simply comical, but the nautical adventure in the tub is one of the most dramatic in the book. Our view, looking past the large foreshortened form of the duck toward George and his vigorous firing away from his boat in full sail, recalls similar compositions in nautical battle paintings, and in battleship comic books. The mock-heroic nature of this image and several others like it is what sets the tone for the book. Throughout the tale, George is undeterred by his absurd tininess and staunchly carries out his parents' directives. These tasks, which would be quite routine and easy if he were his normal size, are ridiculously glorious achievements for a three-inch-high boy.

In the next pair of pictures he cleans up his room (dragging huge toy soldiers), then slides down the banister to get his "little" brother. The next spread gives us the kitchen scene where George gorges himself on an immense cake and a towering soft drink, then does the dishes by skiing down them on a sponge. The next pair of images puts George and his brother at the edge of the house taking out the trash and then frightening the cat. Next, two "shots" give us a subtly interrelated "wildlife" sequence where we first see a heroically caped George confronting a frog as big as he is followed by an inside-the-house scene of George feeding the goldfish while riding one of them. The rest of the book features the sequence of flying-the-toy-airplane scenes and the concluding parental-return scenes.

George Shrinks refers to a wide range of movie genres and specific films. Among the horror-film influences, *The Incredible Shrinking Man* is the most vividly present, but images derived from *King Kong* peek through here and there. Direct references to famous paintings are not numerous in *George Shrinks*, which stays close to its overriding B-movie and picture-book origins, although there is the joking insertion of a print of Georges Seurat's *Sunday Afternoon on the Island of La Grande Jatte*. This reduced version of a famous "Georges" painting hangs just above the shrunken version of George, the protagonist, as he slides down the banister.

Picture-book traditions are key. Foremost among the picture-book influences are Maurice Sendak's *Where the Wild Things Are* and *In the Night Kitchen*. The unflappable courage George exhibits as he faces a monstrously large world suggests the similar pluckiness of Max as he faces down the wild things in their wild place and Mickey as he bravely rises up from his almost baking in the oven of the night kitchen. Furthermore, several of Joyce's airplane images in *George Shrinks* refer directly to the images of Mickey in flight over his night kitchen. Joyce also looks through Sendak toward Winsor Mc-Cay, whose Little Nemo's visits to dreamland are precursors to both Mickey's and George's antics. McCay's role as a pioneer in the development of film animation makes him an important ancestor for Joyce. We shall see further McKay echoes—especially in *Dinosaur Bob* and *Santa Calls*.

In this as well as other books Joyce orchestrates a mélange of elements he enjoys in the works of others. His books are not so much derivative as they are recombinative: He makes something strikingly original by eloquently reshuffling familiar motifs and enlivening the whole with his distinctively personal antic energy. One small but interestingly clever element in *George Shrinks* that shows Joyce's compositional and narrative ingenuity is his use of the eyes of toy figures to direct the gaze of the viewer. Compositional use of eyes is a standard device of the visual arts, of course, but Joyce gives it a new twist by arranging his scenes so that the eyes of the teddy bear, the toy soldiers, and the other toy figures are always aimed toward George's activities. The lively dynamic of the watching toys is handled with verisimilitude in each individual scene, so that the toys seem only accidentally to be providing meaningful glances. The consistently bemused witnessing by the toys contributes to the aliveness of each image without at any point seeming to violate our understanding that the toys are inanimate objects.

Bently & Egg (1992)

As we have seen, the heroic exploits and nonchalant courage of George are those of the staunch Sendakian child. In *Bently & Egg*, however, we have a hero of another sort—a swashbuckling figure out of the old movies. Curiously the world this unlikely hero swashbuckles through seems derived from a very uncinematic source, the books of Beatrix Potter. The dashing (and swinging-from-ropes-and-chandeliers) film hero—as exemplified by Douglas Fairbanks as Zorro and D'Artagnan or Errol Flynn as Robin Hood[2] and Captain Blood—is one sort of model for Bently's heroic rescue of Egg, but the visual vocabulary for such active heroics can be found in adventure films of every stripe, including cowboy flicks. The film *Around the World in Eighty Days* is evoked by Bently's gallant balloon-riding-rescue antics. The low-angle, dramatic compositions that image most of Bently's heroics bear resemblance to movie posters and comic-book images—in particular, Bently's scenes are suggestive of the high drama of comic-book covers, where striking compositions have always been greatly valued because hyperdramatic cover designs can arrest the attention of the potential purchaser.

The publication of *The World of William Joyce Scrapbook* in 1997 has made available to us an intimate view of Joyce's preoccupations and working methods. For instance, the *Scrapbook* shows us that the composition of one of the more striking pictures in *Bently & Egg*, the illustration of Bently lassoing Egg in cowboy fashion, is based on an arrangement of objects on Joyce's studio desktop. A photograph on page 26 of the *Scrapbook* shows us the objects posed for the picture; the three-monkey bookend, the books, the phone, the egg, and the chair are in the exact positions they occupy in the finished illustration. In the spot where we see Bently in the finished illustration a toy cowboy with lasso stands as the central figure. The juxtaposition of the illustration and its prototype photo shows that Joyce achieves striking toy's-eye-view compositions by providing himself with views from such positions. It is clear, too, that the careful use of models for objects plays a role in Joyce's production of images.

Bently & Egg demonstrates Joyce's artistic versatility. Painted just two years after *A Day with Wilbur Robinson*, it is handled in an entirely different style. The pale pastel colors and treatment of the animal characters suggest the influence of Beatrix Potter. In particular, the personality and the fastidious, gentlemanly manner of Bently recalls Potter's frog character Jeremy Fisher. With regard to the plot there are other echoes. Bently's fearless wild rides recall Toad of *Wind in the Willows*, and the egg-minding plot of *Bently & Egg* is a familiar one that looks back to the egg sitting of a Margaret Wise Brown rabbit (in *The Golden Egg Book*) and Dr. Seuss's elephant nesting (in *Horton Hatches the Egg*). There is also an abandoned-toy motif that recalls *The Velveteen Rabbit* and a use of poem composition as a means to comment on the moment that recalls a similar strategy used in the whimsical development of Winnie the Pooh's self-preoccupied escapades. That *Bently & Egg* is a compendium of sources in no way diminishes the distinction of this lovely book; its originality lies in the way Joyce energizes variations on familiar plots and images by means of striking compositions, embedding all elements in a movie-plot-derived, action-packed sequence of incidents. As Bently moves in a left to right, swashbuckling slash of movement, we are made to share his wild frame-by-frame progression. The willingness to try new styles and the care in composition evident in *Bently & Egg* signaled a new level of ambitious artistry that was to achieve further expression in *Santa Calls*. Joyce has said *Santa Calls* took two years.

Santa Calls (1993)

Art Aimesworth of *Santa Calls* resembles the heroes of series novels. He is somewhat like a Hardy boy or a Nancy Drew, but Art's preoccupation with inventions makes him, most of all, a hero in the mold of Tom Swift. On the surface the plot follows a heroic, Tom Swift pattern, but underlying the young-inventor-as-crime-fighter tale is the family matter of his sister Esther's desire for respect. The heroic action is presented as a somewhat inflated and mock-heroic chronicle, with the "real" tale involving Art's simple discovery of the value of his sister. The whole adventure is, in fact, Santa's present to Esther.

The most important single popular-culture influence is Winsor McCay's comic strip *Little Nemo in Slumberland.* McCay's classic strips from around 1905 to 1908 had been revived and partially republished by the time Joyce was working on *Santa Calls.* Some images in Joyce's North Pole resemble the images of two of the dream palaces lavishly depicted in McCay's strip—those of King Morpheus and of Jack Frost. It is possible that Joyce sets his Santa tale in the year 1908 to underscore the connection with the strange dreams of Winsor McCay.[3] The Sendak inspiration comes into play here also because of the much-discussed influence of McCay's slumberland world on Sendak's *In The Night Kitchen*, which, as we saw earlier, was also a source of imagery for Joyce's *George Shrinks.* Joyce's use of high drama, night-time lighting, and the notion of a densely populated North Pole city probably owes something to Chris Van Allsburg's *Polar Express*, but Van Allsburg's austerely black-and-white, twilight-zone North Pole is very different in visual style and tone from Joyce's brightly colorful phantasmagoria. Film influences on *Santa Calls* include *Babes in Toyland* and Busby Berkeley musicals. Again, there is much use of powerful low-angle shots of spectacular, often up-in-the-air, heroics.

Some of the most spectacular scenes in *Santa Calls* seem inspired by Italian Renaissance art—especially the paintings of Venetian master Tintoretto, who was adept at dynamic images of bodies flying through space and elaborate scenes of assembly, presentation, and rescue. The central images in *Santa Calls*, in which the children are being presented toward raised platforms on which Santa and Mrs. Claus stand facing throngs of onlookers, recalls such Tintoretto compositions as *St. Mark Rescuing a Slave, Presentation of the Virgin in the Temple*, and *Christ before Pilate.* Whether or not Joyce was conscious of paralleling Tintoretto's heroic religious paintings, it is instructive to make the comparison to appreciate the visual grandeur of the images in this most epic of Joyce's books.

The Leaf Men and the Brave Good Bugs (1996)

The Leaf Men and the Brave Good Bugs resembles *Santa Calls* in its coupling of an entertainingly heroic action and a strong undercurrent of family feeling. Depicting the Leaf Men characters gives Joyce another opportunity to indulge his love of old-fashioned-adventure-movie swashbuckling in the Errol Flynn mold. The stance, behavior, and rhetoric of these handsome elfin heroes are pure Robin Hood. The Brave Good Bugs are stalwart little hobbit-like creatures that solicit the saving of the day by their earnest, well-intentioned efforts, despite their lack of swashbuckling skills.

Joyce has described this as his favorite of all his books (*Scrapbook*, 40), though it is doubtful many of his fans would share this preference. The yearning of the old woman for the love of her long-lost parents is sentimental in ways that the humor and artistic razzle-dazzle of the book cannot completely redeem.

The toy man who becomes the agent for the old woman's remembrance and recovery is, however, a wonderful device visually, with his metallic-tuxedo toy glamour. There is a strange beauty to the scene where the toy man is carried, pallbearer style, across the old woman's bed as she sleeps. The toy figure is silhouetted against moonlit clouds, while Leaf Men and Bugs gaze in with concern through the open window. It is a lovely fulfillment of the book's wishful belief in goodly sprites and a motto that says "the garden is a miraculous place, and anything can happen on a beautiful moonlit night." Although this book, unlike other Joyce works, fails to counterbalance its sentiment sufficiently with humor, it is a strong confirmation of his appreciation for family bonds.

ECCENTRIC FAMILIES

The next five books under discussion reverse the pattern evident in the previous four. Whereas *George Shrinks*, *Bently & Egg*, *Santa Calls*, and *The Leaf Men* unfold their plots as heroic actions while presenting family feelings as underlying sentiments and punch lines, the next set—*Dinosaur Bob*, *A Day with Wilbur Robinson*, *Buddy*, *Rolie Polie Olie*, and *The World of William Joyce Scrapbook*—are expositions of the antics of families with scattered instances of heroic or mock-heroic action serving as gags within the overall vaudeville of the eccentric household. Joyce's eccentric-family books tend toward the variety-show structure. Although *Dinosaur Bob* and *Buddy* do have plots, after a fashion, the emphasis, even in those works, is more on the one-after-another staging of the antics than on structuring a narrative.

The culture of the family from the child's angle of vision is basic to Joyce's works. The kid's point of view is specifically that of a grownup kid named William Joyce. Several of Joyce's books testify to the wonderful grandeur of families that can manage to be eccentric. Although one of the models for his use of the oddball family motif seems to be the penniless, good-hearted Sycamore family from *You Can't Take It with You*, the Frank Capra film based on the Kaufman and Hart play—pennilessness is not part of the context in any of Joyce's eccentric family pieces. In fact, the odd behaviors of Joyce's lovable clans are often made possible by their riches. Joyce's eccentric families have the benign wealth of Daddy Warbucks of the *Little Orphan Annie* cartoons or of the Rich family of the *Richie Rich* comic books.

Dinosaur Bob and His Adventures with the Family Lazardo (1988)

Joyce's first eccentric-family tale is in many respects his most remarkable. *Dinosaur Bob and His Adventures with the Family Lazardo* gives us an elegantly mansion-ensconced doctor, wife, son, and two daughters, who make a habit of unusual vacations from which they bring back surprising things. Finding a brontosaurus during an expedition to Africa, they decide to adopt it as a pet and bring it home to their suburban estate in "Pimlico Hills."

Although some commentators have identified the setting of *Dinosaur Bob* as the 1930s—one critic calls it "an appealing homage to the 1930s" (Dirda, 10)—Joyce is quite specific about the year, declaring on the end-paper map illustration that "This is 1929 ya know!" One can also note that a movie theater marquee in one of the Pimlico Hills images advertises a movie called *Girl Chasers of 1929*. It is important to the positive aura of the Lazardos that we see them as a fun family of the Jazz Age, rather than as an isolate moneybags clan of the Depression. The Roaring Twenties connection is reinforced by the clothing, hairstyles, car designs, and the names of two of the kids—who are dubbed Scotty and Zelda to remind us of Jazz Age literary lights, F. Scott and Zelda Fitzgerald. The story is set at the last possible moment of the glorious 1920s when almost anything, including a dinosaur who can play "The Hokey Pokey" on a trumpet, still seems possible.

Between the lines of this bizarrely gorgeous book, Joyce presents a warmly affectionate view of a family unit. Here is a family whose vacations are a source of joy. They carry a globe with them and decide and revise their travel plans by happy impulse. So open to divergent changes in itinerary are the Lazardos that, once the redoubtable Bob makes his appearance, all plans reorganize around their newfound prehistoric pal. A voyage down the Nile on the back of Bob is followed by a Bob-centered, ocean-liner voyage home. The story that underlies this visual feast is slight, but at its heart resides a family ruled by the childish inclination to say yes to the most unlikely of possibilities. Among the factors that make *Dinosaur Bob* such a kick for kids are the double satisfactions of eccentric impulse and complete confidence; the parental characters are as fully ruled by a childlike attitude as their children are, and the tale projects a strong confidence that the childlike attitude is absolutely the right approach. There is never any doubt that the ending will be happy and that the Lazardos' ridiculous willingness to adopt a pet larger than their mansion will work out well.

Influences on *Dinosaur Bob* obviously include the numerous books about dinosaurs that Joyce devoured as a boy and that he claims to have recycled in his elementary school drawings (*Scrapbook*, 8). Old-fashioned dinosaur toys determine much of the look of this brontosaurus-like animal. *King Kong* is the film of most important influence on this picture tale. The plot roughly parallels the capture-a-huge-creature-in-the-jungle-then-have-him-run-amuck-in-the-American-city motif made famous in *Kong* (*Scrapbook*, 42). Joyce also points out that other great American legends of ridiculous heroic largeness, such as the Paul Bunyan tales, also contributed to his conception (*Scrapbook*, 8). Other cinematic and historical references include tiny cameo appearances by figures that resemble such characters as Noel Coward, Otto Preminger, and Babe Ruth. The concluding events of *Dinosaur Bob* resemble the typical sports-movie climax.

The influence of Winsor McCay on *Dinosaur Bob* can be assumed. McCay's pioneering animated film *Gertie the Dinosaur* featured an amiable brontosaurus much like Joyce's Bob. Joyce makes an explicit connection to Harold Gray's *Little Orphan Annie* comic strip through the similar treatment of speechless turbaned helpers: Jumbu, who works for the Lazardos, is suggestive of Punjab, the loyal assistant of Daddy Warbucks. The visual-arts influences include N. C. Wyeth and Maxfield Parrish. The striking use of color suggests both these artists. The vivid blue skies with puffy white clouds seem particularly suggestive of Parrish. The look of the building-lined streets of the town bring to mind such Edward Hopper works as *Early Sunday Morning*, which was painted, appropriately enough, in the year 1930. Grant Wood is a key influence on the toylike depiction of human figures in many of Joyce's books, including this one, and the influence of Wood's swelling landscapes and bulbous trees can be seen in the scene where Dinosaur Bob rides a train.

Joyce's whimsicality has a friendliness to it that makes clear that this absurd world is not bent on the destruction of its inhabitants. The forms of his books are intentionally constructed to comfort. Joyce has confirmed that he prefers rounded forms because of the pleasures and comforts they offer his audiences (Conversations). The strong connection to Grant Wood serves a double purpose in *Dinosaur Bob*—evoking the feel of America in the late 1920s–early 1930s and providing the book's world with a pleasurable shapeliness.

A Day with Wilbur Robinson (1990)

The eccentric-family motif receives expanded treatment in *A Day with Wilbur Robinson*, the next self-illustrated book Joyce did after *Dinosaur Bob* (1988). The styles of the two books are, indeed, quite similar. Although the colors are somewhat more muted in *Wilbur Robinson* in comparison with those of *Dinosaur Bob*, the stylistic resemblances are such that one could almost feel that the Lazardos and Robinsons might be neighbors. The historic period is vaguely treated, but it is made relatively clear in one view from the Robinson's backyard in which an automobile, identifiable as belonging to the late forties or early fifties, is visible.

The ample visual wit of *A Day with Wilbur Robinson* more than makes up for the book's lack of plot. As with the best work of Randolph Caldecott, Joyce's *Wilbur Robinson* rewards the attentive "reader" with countless small visual delights. More often than not the plain, understated text is counterpointed in bizarre ways by depicted absurdities. The words fall hilariously and intentionally short of doing justice to the events shown in the scenes. Many gags residing entirely in the images are not referred to directly in the words. The text is a bland first-person narration by a boy who has gone visiting at his friend Wilbur's house. It seems quite appropriate that the young man, who looks to be about nine years old, is giving us so few words of description and commentary; the narration has a naturally boyish flavor, as if it were a brief account for a letter home or a school composition.

Starting with the arrival at the front door of the Robinson house, the narrator tells us that he has "said hello to the twin uncles, Dmitri and Spike," but gives us no explanation as to why the twins appear to be dwelling in large flower pots, one on each side of the door. We overhear Wilbur say that "Lefty will take your bag," but we must look carefully at this page and the one following to grasp that Lefty—who is never seen in his entirety anywhere in the book, despite the appearances of parts of him in almost every scene—is a gigantic octopus. Another silly subtlety observable at the front door are the tiny uniformed birds, never referred to in the text, but frequently seen throughout. These birds would seem to be the explanation of how Wilbur always knows of the narrator's arrival even before he knocks. (Yes, a little bird tells him.)

Our first glimpse of the inside of the house in the next image is accompanied by several exercises in understatement. We are told that "Aunt Billie was playing with her train set, Cousin Pete was walking the cats, and Uncle Gaston sat comfortably in the family cannon." The words lack excitement, but the picture tells us that the "train set" is an enormous locomotive, "the cats" are three full-grown tigers, and "the family cannon" is a major piece of artillery.

The next image takes us into the backyard where Wilbur's father is inexplicably using a metal detector to look for Grandfather's false teeth (and Grandfather). Mr. Robinson is assisted by Carl the robot, who is digging holes in the yard according to the dictates of the metal detector. The contents of these holes are presented as hilariously silly archaeological excavations; perhaps the funniest of these digs reveals a gigantic (presumably prehistoric) frog skull that is wearing a little top hat, which has to be a reference to the 1955 Warner Brothers cartoon *One Froggy Evening* in which an infinitely excavated frog sings and dances to the ruination of the poor schmucks who dig him up. The play and counterplay of all this delightful goofiness makes this book a pleasure to reread. It is possible to see new things at every return visit to the Robinson mansion.

References to *King Kong* constitute a running gag in this and many of Joyce's other books. In one of the interior scenes, Wilbur's sister Blanche is seen "modeling her new prom dress," which is topped off with a hat that makes her look like a rendition of the Empire State Building with a tiny King Kong, assaulted by airplanes, climbing up the side. Joyce tells us that *King Kong* was his favorite movie when he was growing up (*Scrapbook*, 42). Affection for this classic film ape has led Joyce to include Mr. Kong as an understated signature element in many of his books. Kong is not as relentlessly included as the bull terrier unfailingly repeated in Chris Van Allsburg's books, but Kong does often show up in Joyce's pictures.

A comment on the jacket cover of *A Day with Wilbur Robinson* describes it as "a thickly disguised" account of William Joyce's childhood, and Joyce has mentioned that he derived the bizarre goings-on at the Robinson mansion from memories of his childhood combined with appealing bits and pieces of popular culture.

> *A Day with Wilbur Robinson* is about a lot of things that actually happened to me when I was a kid. My dad was always finding really cool stuff with his metal detector; my uncle told me he was from outer space; my grandfather had false teeth that were always getting lost; my sister paid me to feed her grapes while she talked to her boyfriend on the phone; and our dog was blind. (I gave her glasses in the book.) The kid down the street from me lived in a big grand house.... His house was really fun to visit. So I mixed all these things up with some of my favorite movies like *Tarzan* and *The Swiss Family Robinson* and *Bringing Up Baby* and *Earth vs. the Flying Saucers*, and what I ended up with was a book about a normal kid who spends the night at this amazing house filled with robots and animals and really interesting people. (*Scrapbook*, 23)

Remarks of this sort in Joyce's *Scrapbook* reveal the extent to which he has consciously woven popular-culture motifs into his books. He is, however, selective in the motifs he mentions, tending to accentuate what he sees as "fun" allusions.

Buddy: Based on the True Story of Gertrude Lintz (1997)

According to comments Joyce makes in the *Scrapbook*, it was a commission to "write" a movie that stimulated the creation of *Buddy*. He does not make clear the sequence of events, but it appears that he was a prime mover in the writing of the screenplay as well as the book (*Scrapbook*, 42).

Although *Buddy* is based on "the true story of Gertrude Lintz" as narrated in her book *Animals Are My Hobby*, the way events unfold in the absurdly nonfictional *Buddy* resembles in many respects the way events unfold in the absurdly fictional *Dinosaur Bob*. In *Buddy* Joyce deftly blends his impulse toward the fantastic with his reinvention of the life and times of the Lintz family.[4]

The Lintz's of the 1930s, like the Lazardos of 1929, are wealthy mansion dwellers. In both cases, the fabulous wealth appears to be partly inherited and partly due to the success of the husband's medical practice. The Lintz household has the same sort of comaraderie and sense of fun as the Lazardo family, but the nature of the clan is quite different. The Lintz "family" is mostly animals—a gorilla, two chimpanzees, a leopard, a parrot, a komodo dragon, a dachshund, and two servants, in addition to the ostensible "parents," Gertie and Dr. Bill. The year in which *Buddy* begins is almost the same as the year of *Dinosaur Bob* when we calculate that Buddy came to the Lintz's approximately three years before the 1933 World's Fair.

We can also find resemblance between the Lintz mansion and the eccentric big house of the Wilbur Robinson family. Each of the Lintz animals is an eccentric by its very nature, and these zoological oddities are seen to cavort on the croquet field in the early pages of the book in ways that somewhat suggest the hijinks we witnessed at the Robinson mansion. The odd similarities include the fact that both households have dogs that wear eyeglasses. A large pet gorilla may not be as bizarre as a gigantic pet octopus, but it is bizarre enough for a book that purports to be nonfictional.

Despite its farcical elements the story of Buddy's eccentricities goes beyond the comical. In the climax of the story Buddy's hysterical fear of water revives the wild animal in him, and there is briefly a danger that he may seriously harm his adoptive human mother. This turn of events eventually leads to a satisfying conclusion with Buddy loosed in a large gorilla park at a zoo where the Lintz menagerie will be allowed to visit him regularly.

Buddy the book and *Buddy* the film have many striking differences. The opening segment of the film takes advantage of its visual medium to maximize the eccentricities of the animal household. The chimpanzees, in particular, get to do many silly and vivid things in the movie; in the book they are largely helpful and benign—much like the lovingly good children of the Lazardo family. Also, despite the simplified nature of the storytelling in the book, the Gertrude Lintz we find there is more complex and satisfying than her film counterpart. For instance, in the book Gertrude is the one who has the prudent doubts about the safety of taking Buddy to the World's Fair, but in the film it is always her doctor husband who provides the voice of caution. By keeping both the hopes about the apes and the fears about them as separate parts of Gertrude's attitude, Joyce makes Gertrude a more interesting and wiser person. The disadvantage is that the apparently mindless husband of Joyce's book seems to be as one-dimensional as a cartoon character and rather unworthy of his dynamic wife.

I am probably not the only one who finds the stylish 1930s-era images and anecdotes of the book much more attractive work than the film's endless sequences of Hollywood-enhanced chimpanzee mischief. The chimps are funny, but the endless slapstick of their misbehaviors in the film distracts us from the ensemble of the Lintz household, which is orchestrated to such fine advantage in the book. It is, at any rate, to the book we must turn for Joyce's definitive version. The book is, in fact, more rich in cinematic possibilities than the current film version is able to realize. The look of the book is clearly influenced by films of the twenties, thirties, and forties; and it should be noted that *Buddy* gave Joyce unusually rich opportunities to play with allusions to one of his favorite movies, *King Kong*. Perhaps Joyce will someday have an opportunity to do an animated version of *Buddy* that will bring this charming tale more fully to the screen. Although the interior illustrations of the book version of *Buddy* are in reddish monochrome pastels rather than full color paintings, the visual style is quite similar to that of *Dinosaur Bob* and, once again, owes much to the toylike and smoothly rounded world of the paintings of Grant Wood.

Rolie Polie Olie (1999)

In 1999 Joyce began to contribute directly to the common culture of Saturday morning TV through a television show called *Rolie Polie Olie*. In this animated situation comedy, which has also been developed into a series of picture books, Joyce takes his love of rounded forms and of eccentric yet blissfully happy families to another sort of extreme. The sweetly conventional nature of this weirdly rendered family makes it more eccentric in appearance than in substance, but it is something of an achievement that Joyce has been able to replace his traditional illustrator's techniques with computer graphic methods that lend visual excitement to this revival of the world of *Leave It To Beaver* and *Father Knows Best*. Through his *Rolie* TV series and books Joyce manages to suggest in a back-to-basics way that the old-fashioned sitcoms were not without their points, with the central one being that, in the long run, it is not a bad thing for quirky families to be bound together by unembarrassed love. Many readers and viewers will find *Rolie Polie Olie* more than a tad too sweet to admire, despite its almost maniacal intensity and its "living" furniture suggestive of *Peewee's Playhouse* and early *Betty Boop* cartoons; but as an experiment in graphic style, it is further evidence of Joyce's knack for reinventing the familiar.

There is the danger, however, that the double appeal to adults and children that Joyce's best books could get lost in the shuffle of the Rolie Polie craze. For all their amazing graphic interest the sweet cuteness of books such as *Rolie Polie Olie* and *Snowie Rolie* will not hold on to the adult half of the audience. One hopes that Joyce's *Rolie* works will not parallel the situation of the program *Sesame Street*, which in its prime years balanced the witty vaudeville of such characters as Bert and Ernie and Kermit the Frog against the sweetness of Big Bird, but that seems increasingly, in recent years, to have plunged down the slippery, infantile slope of "Hug-Me-Elmo."

The World of William Joyce Scrapbook (1997)

Joyce's childhood family life has obviously figured prominently in his books, but he has also written a book that devotes considerable attention to the eccentricities of his life as a parent. *The World of William Joyce Scrapbook* is a useful resource for background information about the artist's development, working methods, and attitudes toward the world and his art, but it also devotes considerable space to the story of his life in the 1990s, as the father character in his very own eccentric family. In his *Scrapbook* Joyce shows himself to be almost as zany as a dad as he is as an artist.

Joyce's playfulness emerges primarily in conjunction with holidays. For the Fourth of July he organizes the neighborhood to set up fortresses constructed of styrofoam and other light materials and furnishes these constructions with thousands of toy soldiers as well as innumerable flags, barricades, and so forth. When all is elaborately readied, implanted fireworks are set off to destroy the hapless toy armies.

Joyce's embrace of Halloween is equally enthusiastic and involves a makeover of the family home.

Halloween is maybe my favorite holiday. I take the whole month of October off and decorate the house. Every year my next-door neighbors and I build some really spooky stuff—we've made 20-foot skeletons and a 30-foot spider. I've got over 100 skeletons in my closets, so we haul those all out, and paint the living-room walls with Halloween murals. (*Scrapbook*, 30)

Yet his head-over-heels involvement in Christmas is no less massive and involves a repainting of the interior of his house with snowflakes and other appropriate imagery. It goes without saying, of course, that Easter with its opportunities for egg painting is also a big event for the Joyce family. The egg-painting enthusiasm of the frog protagonist of *Bently & Egg* is one expression of Joyce's passion for that holiday.

Looking at Joyce family photos and reading Joyce's recountings of his holiday spiritedness, one wonders how he finds time amidst his holiday preparations and heavy schedule of family activities to do his books. One suspects that he is a high-energy person who finds his work and his play to be two aspects of the same impulse. Looking at photos of Joyce cavorting with his kids at the beach, it is easy to see why the eccentric families of his books are not that difficult for him to imagine. One suspects that if Joyce and family encountered a real dinosaur they would be just as ready as the Lazardos to adopt an unusually large pet (*Scrapbook*, 27–33).

CONCLUSION

The delight that Joyce takes in holidays brings us back to the concept of a common culture mentioned at the beginning of this essay. Joyce's wholehearted celebration of the pantheon of America's popular culture makes the whimsical faith that lies behind the famous slogan "Yes, Virginia, there is a Santa Claus" into a "religion" that is always tongue-in-cheek but never cynical. Joyce's attitude is childlike in the best sort of way. He revels in the play opportunities provided by America's adoration of the pseudo "deities" that dominate our shared popular culture. His dashing heroes, like those of the silver screen, project an air of casual invulnerability—a godlike manner that has much in common with the attitude of the child at play. Neither Errol Flynn nor the American version of Robin Hood he portrays are godlike in any really religious way, but there is room in our world for adopting a playful worshipfulness toward what the actor and the characters he acts combine to create.

In a not yet published series of books, described in the *Scrapbook*, Joyce promises to deliver a full pantheon of folk figures from the lore of bedtime tales. The Sandman, Jack Frost, the Man in the Moon, and the Tooth Fairy will all make appearances in books about "The Guardians of Childhood." He plans to establish a team of household gods that have something to do with Mount Olympus on the one hand and DC Comics' Justice League on the other.

It seems likely that Joyce's works will continue to carry on the hopeful playfulness that is crucial to the life of our common culture. It is a culture that does not segregate traditional folklore and mythology from the parallel concoctions of the various entertainment industries. Joyce's cheerfully postmodern common culture accepts it all—whether it comes by television, movie screen, oil painting, comic book, dime novel, picture book, advertising slogan, or whatever. Because Joyce loves to be silly (but is nobody's fool) and because he has developed ways to capture the wonders of fantasy in glorious extravagances of illustration and wise minimalisms of wittily chosen words, he seems capable of becoming an artistic high priest (and low priest) of our common culture. He confirms for readers of all ages the value of the childlike view and seems to suggest, through the infusion of real bravery and antic swashbuckling into the midst of the family adventure, that having fun and being heroic have much in common with each other and mysteriously reinforce the affectionate loyalties that hold families together.

The value of Joyce's best work lies in the excellence of his art more than in the archaeology of his images, but it is interesting and valuable that Joyce has found ways to make popular-culture traditions count as traditions in exactly the same way as fine-arts traditions. Because Joyce is so open and multifarious in his borrowings he presents a valuable opportunity to witness how all sorts of traditions can flow together to invigorate the literary-visual forms of picture books.

NOTES

1. Parallels to Maurice Sendak's *In the Night Kitchen* and Winsor McCay's *Little Nemo in Slumberland* might seem to indicate that George is dreaming, but parallels to fairy tales of tiny boys and the science-fiction film *The Incredible Shrinking Man* suggest that George is strangely transformed in a "real" world. I asked Joyce about this and he confirmed that, indeed, he wanted to leave the reader in some doubt with regard to the reality versus dream question, even though he left small visual clues that George's shrinkage happened in reality (Conversations).

2. Joyce has mentioned in several places that he is a big fan of Robin Hood. He seems to have in mind classic illustrations by both N. C. Wyeth and Howard Pyle.
3. In 1976 Dover Publications reprinted a number of sequences of McCay's *Little Nemo in Slumberland* in full color. Included were episodes featuring the palaces of King Morpheus and Jack Frost.
4. Joyce adapts and condenses the Lintz material in numerous ways. In actuality, for instance, Gertrude Lintz had two gorillas. In addition to Buddy there was Masa, and some of the things that happened to Buddy in Joyce's book happened to Masa in the Lintz memoirs. Furthermore, Joyce's peaceable-kingdom-like account of the Lintz menagerie does not take into account the more brutal behaviors and tendencies of certain of her animals—her leopard and her "Chinese dragon," for instance.

WORKS CITED

Bourne, Geoffrey, and Maury Cohen. *The Gentle Giants: The Gorilla Story*. New York: Putnam's, 1975.

Brown, Margaret Wise. *The Golden Egg Book*. Illus. Leonard Weisgard. New York: Simon & Schuster, 1947.

Cech, John. "A Palette of Picture Books." *The Washington Post Book World*. November 10, 1985: 19, 22.

Dirda, Michael. "Dinosaur Bob." *The Washington Post Book World*. October 9, 1988: 10–11.

Geisel, Theodore (Dr. Seuss). *Horton Hatches the Egg*. New York: Random House, 1940.

Grahame, Kenneth. *The Wind in the Willows*, 1908.

Hart, Moss, and George Kaufman. *You Can't Take It with You*. New York: Dramatist Play Service, 1937.

Joyce, William. *Bently & Egg*. New York: HarperCollins, 1992.

———. *Buddy: Based on the True Story of Gertrude Lintz*. New York: HarperCollins, 1997.

———. Conversations with Joseph Stanton in Honolulu, June 13–14, 2002.

———. *A Day with Wilbur Robinson*. New York: Harper, 1990.

———. *Dinosaur Bob and His Adventures with the Family Lazardo*. New York: Harper & Row, 1988.

———. *George Shrinks*. New York: Harper & Row, 1985.

———. *The Leaf Men and the Brave Good Bugs*. New York: HarperCollins, 1996.

———. *Rolie Polie Olie*. New York: HarperCollins, 1999.

———. *Santa Calls*. New York: HarperCollins, 1993.

———. *The World of William Joyce Scrapbook*. New York: HarperCollins, 1997.

Lintz, Gertrude. *Animals Are My Hobby*. New York: McBride & Company, 1942.

McCay, Winsor. *Little Nemo in the Palace of Ice and Further Adventures*. New York: Dover, 1976.

Potter, Beatrix. *Jeremy Fisher.* London: Frederick Warne, 1906.

Pyle, Howard. *The Merry Adventures of Robin Hood*, 1883.

Sendak, Maurice. *In the Night Kitchen.* New York: Harper & Row, 1970.

————. *Where the Wild Things Are.* New York: Harper & Row, 1963.

Seuss, Dr. [Theodore Geisel]. *Horton Hatches the Egg.* New York: Random House, 1940.

Telgen, Diane, ed. *Something About the Author.* Detroit: Gale Research, 1993.

Williams, Marjery. *The Velveteen Rabbit or How Toys Become Real.* Illus. William Nicholson, 1922.

OTHER WORKS OF INTEREST

Gray, Catherine, and James Gray. *Tammy and the Gigantic Fish.* Illus. William Joyce. New York: Harper & Row, 1983.

Joyce, William. Cover illustrations for the following issues of journals: *The New Yorker* for December 12, 1994, September 14, 1998, May 17, 1999, and December 24/31, 2001; *The New York Times Book Review* for December 4, 1994.

Manes, Stephen. *Some of the Adventures of Rhode Island Red.* Illus. William Joyce. New York: Lippincott, 1990.

Maxner, Joyce. *Nicholas Cricket.* Illus. William Joyce. New York: Harper & Row, 1989.

McCay, Winsor. *The Best of Little Nemo in Slumberland.* Ed. Richard Marschall. New York: Stewart, Tabori & Chang, 1997.

Roberts, Bethaney. *Waiting-for-Spring Stories.* Illus. William Joyce. New York: Harper & Row, 1984.

Salinger, Margaretta. *Tintoretto.* New York: Abrams, 1974.

Steer, John. *A Concise History of Venetian Painting.* London: Thames and Hudson, 1970.

Wahl, Jan. *Humphrey's Bear.* Illus. by William Joyce. New York: Holt, 1987.

Winthrop, Elizabeth. *Shoes.* Illus. William Joyce. New York: Harper & Row, 1986.

Surrealism and the Strange Tale in the Picture Books of Chris Van Allsburg

$\mathscr{T}$he picture shows us a darkly lovely rendering of a Venetian canal with two tight rows of buildings facing each other across a narrow waterway. A small arched footbridge delicately links the two sides. But in the background towers a gigantic ocean liner crashing its way into the far end of the canal. On a facing page is the title of the image, *Missing in Venice*, and a caption: "Even with her mighty engines in reverse, the ocean liner was pulled further and further into the canal." Here indeed is a mystery—and a mystery that remains unsolved, because the single picture with its title and caption are all we have. Chris Van Allsburg's collection *The Mysteries of Harris Burdick* is, in fact, a collection of fourteen unsolvable, but intriguingly captioned, mystery pictures. According to the tongue-in-cheek introduction, these images, along with their titles and captions, were left by a man supposedly named Harris Burdick with a children's book editor supposedly named Peter Wenders. Harris Burdick and the manuscripts for which each of the images is just a sample were, of course, never seen again, leaving us with fourteen inscrutable fragments.

In interviews Van Allsburg has resisted attempts to pin down the origins and purposes of his picture-story ideas. He has indicated that he, too, finds his books mysterious and cannot offer simple explanations as to where and how they originate.

> A question I've been asked often is, "Where do your ideas come from?" I've given a variety of answers to this question, such as: "I steal them from the neighborhood kids," "I send away for them by mail order," and "They are beamed to me from outer space." It's not really my intention to be rude or smart-alecky. The fact is, I don't know where my ideas come from. Each story I've written starts out as a vague idea that seems to be going nowhere, then suddenly materializes as a completed concept. It almost seems like a

discovery, as if the story was always there. The few elements I start out with are actually clues. If I figure out what they mean, I can discover the story that's waiting. (Ruello, 169–70)

In this chapter I do not promise to offer definitive solutions to the Harris Burdick mysteries or to any of the other bizarre fancies invented by the mind and art of Chris Van Allsburg. I shall, however, propose a theory concerning the traditions that lie behind his remarkable originality. Van Allsburg's work involves, it seems to me, the yoking together of two kinds of traditions that are almost never discussed together—a popular-culture tradition and an avant-garde, high-modernist tradition.[1] The popular-culture tradition I have in mind will be referred to as the *strangely-enough tale*. The high-art, experimental tradition is, of course, *surrealism*. It too often happens that the popular arts are completely boxed off from the high arts—more often as a result of academic specialization than of overt snobbery—but some of the greatest innovations in the arts come from the surprising mixing of the contents of the various boxes.

Furthermore, because surrealism is a high art with a proclivity for the low, it is of particular importance to understand the ways surrealism can and does connect with popular culture. Also, one should appreciate that, despite the "pastness" of surrealism as a movement of the early to mid-twentieth century, the transaction between surrealism and popular culture continues and flows in both directions: The surrealistically inclined have always appropriated images from popular culture, and popular culture in such forms as magazine advertisements, department-store display windows, and rock videos have often borrowed surrealist procedures and appropriated well-known images from classic surrealist works. As we turn our attention to the children's picture-book genre, we should also bear in mind that, although surrealism is not ordinarily thought of as being aimed at an audience of children, much was made in Breton's manifestos, and in other surrealist documents, of the value of a "childlike" outlook. It is not, therefore, surprising that Van Allsburg, a university-trained fine-arts practitioner working in the popular children's picture-book form, should fuse surrealist and pop-culture motifs. If we can gain some sense of the cultural sources that underlie Van Allsburg's work and the appeal of those elements for audiences of children and adults, we can better appreciate his success, even as we allow his mysteries to remain more or less unsolved.

I begin with a discussion of the several books in which the surrealistic element in Van Allsburg's work can be most clearly seen. I then discuss books that incorporate strangely-enough tales, with attention to how surrealistic and strangely-enough elements coexist in several of Van Allsburg's most distinctive books.

The three books that I discuss as primary examples of the surrealistic tendencies in Van Allsburg's work are *The Mysteries of Harris Burdick*, *Ben's Dream*, and *The Z Was Zapped*. Because the term *surrealism* has been applied in so many ways, I must make clear that the surrealism I have in mind is not primarily the surrealism of Andre Breton and his closest associates. I am not thinking of automatic writing, found objects, random assortments, and frottages. The surrealism that embodies the irrational or nonrational by relying upon the accidental would seem to have little to do with the meticulously designed and arranged works of Van Allsburg. The surrealism I refer to here is the secondary surrealism that derived sustenance, though not methodology, from the liberations effected by Breton and company. I have in mind Giorgio de Chirico,[2] Yves Tanguy, Salvador Dali, Max Ernst, and, most of all, René Magritte. It is, of course, terminologically problematic that these artists did not always fly the surrealist banner. What the works of these artists, as well as the works of Van Allsburg, have in common is that they contain "highly detailed likenesses of objects, straight or distorted, or three-dimensional abstractions, in a fantastic and unexpected juxtaposition, or in a setting of a hallucinatory kind" (Murray and Murray, 402). This kind of surrealism constructs its dream images with a highly self-conscious sense of form and style. The content of the images may arise from the tapping of the subconscious, but the rendering of the work of art is realized with conscious finesse. Van Allsburg's surrealism is quite deliberate, as he himself acknowledges: "If all artists were forced to wear a badge, I'd probably wear the badge of surrealism. I don't mean something as extreme as Salvador Dali's melting clocks, but a gentle surrealism with certain unsettling provocative elements" (Ruello, 169).

Passionate attention to selected likenesses and the employment of unexpected juxtapositions are essential to my three examples of Van Allsburg's surrealism. Perhaps the readiest way to recognize his affiliation with a certain kind of surrealism would be to compare the humorous stage-set images of *The Z Was Zapped* to certain stage-set images of René Magritte. Throughout his career Magritte employed the stage curtain and the shallow space of a stage as a compositional device that gave a theatrical air to his images. The advantages of this performance-evoking strategy include the compositional attractiveness of this mode of display, the basic wittiness of making a static image into a dramatic action, and the effectiveness of this style of presentation as a means of heightening audience attention. Magritte works such as *Homage to Shakespeare* and *Wasted Effort* are particularly amusing in their interplay of landscape and stage-set elements. The metamorphosis of the stage-curtain shape into the fragments of sky we see in both these works is typical of the transformative play Magritte develops in much of his work. Things often turn into sky or stone in Magritte's pictures. Or shoes become feet or bottles become carrots. A complete catalog of Magritte's warpings of one thing into another would be a very long list indeed. Similar transformations could be noted in the works of many other modern artists (and even in the works of some artists of earlier eras), but the clarity and fastidiousness of Magritte's likenesses make him the surrealist forerunner most obviously comparable to Van Allsburg.

In *The Z Was Zapped* many of the letters of the alphabet undergo transformations in keeping with an alliterative phrase utilizing the sound of the letter. Thus we have "The E was slowly Evaporating" as the caption for an on onstage *E* that is fading away at the top as it gives off steam. "The G was starting to Grow" shows rootlike appendages bursting out of the edges of a *G*. Similarly, a *J* is shown to be jittery, an *M* is melting, a *V* is vanishing, and a *W* is warped. Other letters are under attack in a variety of ways. The *B* was bitten, the *C* was cut to ribbons, the *F* was flattened by a gigantic foot, the *K* was kidnapped by gloved hands, the *N* was nailed, the *P* was pecked by a nasty-looking bird, the *Q* was quartered by a knife that hangs in midair without the support of a hand, the *U* was uprooted, the *Y* was yanked, and, of course, the *Z* was zapped. The natural elements play a role in beating up on the hapless alphabet: Lightening zaps the *Z*, an avalanche falls on the *A*, and water soaks the *S*. In addition to the emphasis on absurd transformations of objects, the use of stage settings, and meticulous attention to appearances, Van Allsburg shares with Magritte a knack for witty presentation of body parts (hands and feet in particular) separated from the rest of the body. (The illustrations for *F* and *K* are of interest in this regard.) It is even possible that Van Allsburg, perhaps unconsciously, derived the idea for this book directly from a work by Magritte. Some of the letters that Magritte did as chapter headings for an edition of Lautréamont's *Les chants de Maldoror* are interestingly similar to Van Allsburg's letters. Particularly pertinent is Magritte's drawing of an *R* with an eagle's clawed foot reaching out of one side and a human hand on the other (Hubert, 194–205).

The violence of Van Allsburg's alphabet no doubt comes as a surprise to many readers. The brutal way that many of the letters are destroyed or threatened hardly fits with conventional ideas concerning what is appropriate for small children; although superficially Van Allsburg's transformations may seem more ruthless than Magritte's, there is an element of melodrama to Van Allsburg's staged destructions that makes them, ultimately, less unset-

tling than Magritte's. Although it seems odd that *The Z is Zapped* (an alphabet book ostensibly to be shared with the youngest of children) is in several
respects the least gentle of Van Allsburg's exercises in surrealism, it can be
seen that Van Allsburg's "unsettling provocative elements" are held under
control by our awareness that the artist-writer is having fun with his series
of alphabetic horror shows. While Van Allsburg's *The Z Was Zapped* belongs
to a genre of whimsical nonsense alphabets perhaps best represented by Wal-
ter Crane's *The Absurd ABC*—with its wonderful jumble of motifs from
nursery rhymes and fairy tales—it is the Magritte-like quality of Van Allsburg's ABCs that makes their absurdity distinctive. He has both fulfilled and
transcended the conventions of the alphabet-book genre to create a new sort
of entertainment for parent-child teams of readers.

 Ben's Dream wears the badge of surrealism through the genuinely
dreamlike nature of its narrative. Also suggestive of surrealism is its humorous display of famous monuments and buildings. A specific connection to
surrealism can be found in the obvious echo of an image from *Une semaine
de bonté*, a surrealist montage picture book by Max Ernst.[3] Ernst's image of
the Egyptian Sphinx seen through the window of a railroad car is reinvented
by Van Allsburg in the image of the Sphinx seen from the front porch of
Ben's floating house—in both images the head of the Sphinx is facing exactly the same way. It would not be surprising to hear that Van Allsburg was
directly inspired by the example of Ernst's collage novel (Ernst, 137). Beyond
this specific reference, making famous buildings look ridiculous is entirely in
the spirit of the surrealist project. It should be noted, however, that the punch
line of *Ben's Dream*, which indicates that the boy and the girl had dreamed
the same dream, is suggestive of the strangely-enough motif. Also, although
Ben's Dream can be seen to have derived from surrealism, it is too mild mannered, too gentle in its dreaming to be fully in tune with the disturbing ferocity of the great surrealist masterpieces.

 Surrealist qualities of a more unsettling sort are to be found, however, in *The Mysteries of Harris Burdick*. Van Allsburg's startling intrusion of
an ocean liner into a canal that I referred to at the beginning of this essay
bears a family resemblance to the startling emergence of a train engine
from a fireplace in Magritte's *Time Transfixed*. The playful joining of the
ordinary to the extraordinary are specialities of both Magritte and Van
Allsburg. Van Allsburg gives us an unexceptional suburban street where we
discover one of the houses to be blasting off like a rocket ship, whereas
Magritte gives us a fish washed up on the shore that just happens to have
legs where its tail should be. The Magritte resemblance has been suggested by other commentators on Van Allsburg's books. For instance, John

Russell, reviewing *The Wreck of the Zephyr,* noted that "some of the images of flight are worthy of Magritte himself."

The literary aspect of the *Harris Burdick* book also has a rough equivalence in Magritte. Magritte often made the naming of his paintings into a game separate from the making of the pictures. Much could be said about how this practice helped Magritte put forth the fiction that his pictures were not self-revelatory. Magritte often solicited his literary friends to make up names for his pictures, thereby ensuring a mysterious disjunction between the picture and its label. In one sense Van Allsburg also self-consciously cultivates mystery through the puzzling labels he forces us to connect to the *Harris Burdick* pictures, but the stronger effect of the labels is to demystify the pictures, at least to some extent. Each caption implies a particular kind of story. There would no doubt be much more agreement between stories generated from Van Allsburg's captions than there would be between stories generated from Magritte's often baffling titles.

The fourteen inscrutable fragments that make up *The Mysteries of Harris Burdick* are deft excursions into the fantastic that demonstrate the potential of the picture-book form for combining literary and pictorial means to produce powerful literary-pictorial ends. Perhaps not everyone would agree with me that *The Mysteries of Harris Burdick* is the best of Van Allsburg's many excellent picture books, but I think it is the place to look for an understanding of his profoundly whimsical art. Composed as it is of fragments, *Harris Burdick* shows the artist-writer at play in his workshop.

In this strange workshop, the subgenre that I am calling the strangely-enough tale plays a prominent part. The term *strangely enough* is taken from the title of a popular book of tales published by C. B. Colby in 1959.[4] What made Colby's collection of strange stories exciting for twelve-year-olds of all ages was the attitude he adopted toward the material and expressed in his title. Colby managed to present his brief retellings of startling tales in a manner that suggested they might be true, despite their strangeness. Colby's journalistic plain style of writing was one of the elements that seemed to attest to the truth of the tales. Paradoxically, if Colby had been a better writer, his tales would have seemed more literary and thereby less real.[5] The point is that Colby managed to make many of us want to believe that, strangely enough, something remarkable had *really* happened.

The only claim I am making here for Colby is that his work is typical of the genre and more enduring in its unpretentious appeal than many similar collections that have appeared over the years. *Strangely Enough* is interesting primarily as one of the most popular and widely distributed repackagings of contemporary oral tradition in the medium of print. Whether he knew it or not, Colby was a recorder of contemporary folk legends, primarily of the kind that Jan Harold Brunvand describes as "urban legends." Most of Colby's material appeared first in a newspaper column that he wrote for a number of years. His solicitation of tales for his column was his primary means of tale collection. The newspaper context has long been an important element in the spread and development of modern folk legends, because the inclusion of a tale in a publication dedicated to the reporting of fact tends to reinforce any assertion, however slight and whimsical, that the tale is possibly true.[6]

I have no idea whether Van Allsburg was directly influenced by Colby's book or by any of the numerous other books and comic books that have presented similar "strange tales," but it is apparent that several of Van Allsburg's books and all the tales suggested in the fragments included in *The Mysteries of Harris Burdick* make use of the simple but powerful formula found in folk legends. In such tales there is an ordinary context out of which something extraordinary seems to develop. Journalistic versions of such tales tend to be brief and lacking in the histrionics common in oral presentations. Most such tales take no more than a page and a half to recount. The ordinary situation is explicated in a few paragraphs, the extraordinary aspect is delivered as a kind of punch line. The understated manner of the telling in a newspaper context adds to the plausibility of the tales. Sometimes the situation seems to be falling short of the extraordinary until a chance remark by one of the characters betrays the almost dismissed extraordinariness.

Recognizing the relatedness of Van Allsburg's tales to the journalistic retelling of strangely-enough tales, as exemplified by Colby's *Strangely Enough* collection, provides a way of understanding the reason for Van Allsburg's peculiar flatness of delivery and brevity of exposition, which are among the most distinctive features of his storytelling style. In both Colby and Van Allsburg a flatness of tone and a terseness of narration reinforce the surface plausibility of the tale and stand in striking contrast to the bizarreness of what is taking place. Of course, a critical difference between Van Allsburg's tales and Colby's are the wonderful pictures that Van Allsburg employs to make us witnesses of the strange happenings. The startling contrast between Van Allsburg's dull, though carefully crafted, prose and his extraordinary images operates as a continuous irony. It is key to the tension between the ordinary and the marvelous that is his central subject.

The Garden of Abdul Gasazi is an excellent example of the strangely-enough plot and narrative strategy. In this tale, a little boy named Alan is asked to take care of his neighbor's dog.[7] While Alan is walking the dog, the disobedient animal breaks away and heads into the mysterious garden of the magician

Abdul Gasazi. Gasazi's abhorrence of dogs is posted on a sign that declares "AB-SOLUTELY, POSITIVELY NO DOGS ALLOWED IN THIS GARDEN." When the dis-mayed boy reaches Gasazi's house in the center of the garden, the dog is nowhere in sight. It turns out that Gasazi has either used his magic to transform the dog into a duck or played a clever joke on Alan. The rediscovery at the end of the book that the dog was in possession of Alan's hat, which had been stolen by the duck, sets up a final remark by the neighbor ("Why you bad dog," she said. "What are you doing with Alan's hat?"), which suggests—in fine, under-stated, strangely-enough fashion—that the extraordinary explanation is proba-bly the right one.[8]

In *Jumanji*, Van Allsburg turns away somewhat from the popular-culture tradition of Colby and his kind and draws on the more self-consciously lit-erary tradition that derives from the nineteenth-century weird tales of Edgar Allan Poe and Nathaniel Hawthorne, among others. This tradition has con-tinued to enjoy vigorous life in contemporary works of literary fiction and in films. Among the many writers and filmmakers whose stories fit the mold of the strangely-enough tale are Alfred Hitchcock, Roald Dahl, Ray Brad-bury, and Stephen King. The question of interconnections between the weird tales of the literary tradition and the weird tales collected by journal-ists (such as Colby) and scholarly folklorists (such as Jan Harold Brunvand) is a rich topic that has not been adequately addressed. For my purposes here it does not seem possible to cleanly separate the collected from the crafted with regard to influence on Van Allsburg; they are two sides of the same coin. Even the most carefully crafted of literary weird tales are aimed at popular audiences. Although the simplicity and blandness of Van Allsburg's narration of *Jumanji* suggest the collected tale, the twists of *Jumanji*'s little plot and the ironies it sets up recall, in certain respects, the tales of such popular modern storytellers as Dahl and Hitchcock. The grim little twist at the end, where the dangerous jungle game is found by two little boys who are well known for not following directions, is suggestive of one of Hitchcock's wittily grue-some, unhappy endings. But the somewhat more sophisticated feel of this tale does not conceal the strangely-enough mechanism.

Although I shall not discuss here all the varied graphic techniques Van Allsburg has employed in his books, it is interesting to note that following the appearance of his first book, *The Garden of Abdul Gasazi*, he established a pat-tern of publishing one book per year, and, for each of these yearly produc-tions, his artistic techniques were different. Each of his first set of books, in-cluding all the books of his discussed in this chapter, is an experimental working out of new design and material problems that Van Allsburg has set for himself. Underlying his structures and his choices of picture-making techniques is a sculptural sense that derives from his training and practice as a sculptor. Judging from remarks in interviews, Van Allsburg seems to regard himself—even today, after all his years of success as a picture-book artist—as primarily a fine-arts sculptor who does picture books as something of a sideline. The scene in *The Garden of Abdul Gasazi* where Alan runs through the gate in the hedge to first enter the garden is one of many striking instances of sculptural form in Van Allsburg's work. In that scene, Alan and the two statues that border the gate seem to be three statuary variations on the theme "running boy." The gateway itself seems palpably sculptural. Even the separate leaves and blades of grass possess a certain amount of what philosopher of art Susanne Langer would call "kinetic volume" (Langer, 90). Each of these figurations seems static yet uncannily capable of operating in the viewer's space as well as in the virtual scene. This picture subtly suggests to the viewer that he or she might walk into it. The sculptural palpableness of some of Van Allsburg's pictures offers powerful reinforcement of the strangely-enough element in his work. We are drawn into the spaces of the garden of Abdul Gasazi not simply because his style is realistic but because his sculptural effects break down the barrier between our space and the space of the picture. Van Allsburg's sculptural effects in *The Garden of Abdul Gasazi* evoke a twilight-zone mood and have, at the same time, affinities with the sculptural dimensions of works by Dali, Magritte, and other surrealist artists. Thus the strange tale of popular culture and the dream image of surrealistic modernism are fused in a peculiarly powerful way.

The Wreck of the Zephyr is perhaps the work most completely conceived in the strangely-enough manner. Recounters of such legends often endeavor to add credibility to their accounts by using the framing device of casting the narrator in the role of a visitor to a scene of fantastic events; there he or she encounters a person residing in the place who tells the tale that the narrator presumably does no more than record.[9] There is a twist at the end of *The Wreck of the Zephyr* where we are left with the implication that the narrator was the boy protagonist of the tale he has just told. Van Allsburg sets up this turn of events well. Most readers are probably taken somewhat by surprise when the old man's limping walk and anxiousness to go sailing hint that he was once the boy who flew the Zephyr. As usual in the strangely-enough tale, the truth of the story rests on the presumed credibility of the speaker as an eyewitness.

The Wreck of the Zephyr represents a new direction in Van Allsburg's picture-book art, because it was his first venture into color. Later statements about his experiments with color indicate that he was dissatisfied with the technique he employed in this book. His efforts to blend pastels in ways that would create painted effects were apparently the source of some frustration for him. Whatever difficulties this book may have caused him seem to have been worth enduring; *The Wreck of the Zephyr* presents striking images that might not have been achievable in other ways. For instance, the luminescent greens of the ocean on the jacket of *The Wreck of the Zephyr* could not have been produced with the separate-strokes-of-color technique Van Allsburg used in *The Stranger*.

I have already cited John Russell's comment on the evident Magritte influence on *The Wreck of the Zephyr*. As with many Magritte images, several of Van Allsburg's pictures for this book present key elements as suspended or frozen within the scene. Thus Van Allsburg's flying boats have an eerie silence and a seeming motionlessness that are reminiscent of the gigantic apples or rocks Magritte hangs over seascapes in such paintings as *The Beautiful Truths* or *The Castle in the Pyrenees*. Although we could also link the marine dreams of Van Allsburg with the dramatically lighted nineteenth-century luminist scenes of such artists as Fitz Hugh Lane and Martin Johnson Heade, the overall effect of these pictures is Magritte-like.

The best selling of Van Allsburg's picture books, *The Polar Express*, captures a strangely-enough motif that recurs in many forms in American popular culture. Van Allsburg's explanation of how this story came to him provides a fascinating glimpse into his way of imagining but provides little by way of interpretation.

> When I began thinking about what became *The Polar Express*, I had a single image in mind: a young boy sees a train standing still in front of his house one night. The boy and I took a few different trips on that train, but we did not, in a figurative sense, go anywhere. Then I headed north, and I got the feeling that this time I'd picked the right direction, because the train kept rolling all the way to the North Pole. At that point the story seemed literally to present itself. Who lives at the North Pole? Undoubtedly a ceremony of some kind, a ceremony requiring a child, delivered by a train and would have to be named the Polar Express. (Ruello, 170)

An image that might have been one of the Harris Burdick fragments was developed into a story that resolves itself into a kind of seasonal legend. Although the polar rite of winter around which the story revolves is a product of Van Allsburg's knack for developing fantasy rather than a conscious manipulation of an archetypal motif, the archetypal motif of this strangely-enough tale is not hard to spot. The argument of this tale is the heart-warming contention that "Yes, Virginia, there is a Santa Claus." The movie *Miracle on 34th Street* is, of course, relevant here. The popular-culture nature of this tale makes it no less important than it would be if it were tricked out in the trappings of classical myth. The truth-pretense of the reality of Santa is perhaps the most widely distributed of all American strangely-enough motifs. Santa is the "flying-saucer" belief that parents profess in order to make possible an important family game of ritual affection, gift giving, and seasonal celebration.

We might expect to lose the dangerousness of surrealism in Van Allsburg's embrace of Jolly Old Saint Nick, but when we consider the intrusion of a massive train into a quiet suburban street, the restrainedly demonic nature of Van Allsburg's North Pole with its bizarrely vast snow-covered urban appearance, and the quietly nightmarish hugeness of the crowd of identically dressed elves turned out to hear Santa's speech—when we consider all the elements of this late-night sojourn—we find the surrealist edge of danger subtly implicit. It might even be said that there is something about the visualization of Santa's speech to his army of elves that is darkly reminiscent of the famous Leni Riefenstahl film sequences of Hitler addressing his vastly arrayed storm troopers. Although Santa is treated as an unambiguously benign being in the narrative, there is an unsettling quality to the North Pole scene that adds an aesthetically interesting element of disorientation to the miraculous presence of the godlike Santa figure.

An even more mysterious mythos figures in the strangely-enough notion that lies at the center of *The Stranger*, a work that resonates on a number of levels. Visits by gods among mortals are commonplace in mythic traditions. Not identified as a powerful immortal, the god appears on someone's doorstep. Often such tales are moral fables concerning the importance of offering hospitality to strangers. Van Allsburg's tale follows this pattern but adds the twist that the stranger in his book suffers from amnesia owing to a collision with a car whose driver afterward takes him into his home. The stranger's exact identity remains unexplained, but he is suggestive of Jack Frost, a being responsible for changing the season from warm summer to cool autumn and cold winter. Because of the stranger's amnesia, autumn does not come to the place where he has stopped. The farm family he stays with benefits from the prolonged warm weather that produces a bountiful harvest. Eventually the truth dawns on the stranger, and he departs to return to his appointed rounds.

Of course, as with *Polar Express*, we can link the story in *The Stranger* to a variety of popular works that share its basic strangely-enough premise. In a number of recent films a godlike personage intrudes into ordinary lives. Most often these beings are presented as aliens from other worlds, but they are typically given Christ-like qualities of spirituality and innocence, as well as certain amazing powers, that mark them as something above and beyond.

The cult classic science-fiction novel *Stranger in a Strange Land* by Robert Heinlein fits this profile, as do the films *Starman, ET, Man Facing Southeast, Brother from Another Planet, Edward Scissorhands,* and *Wings of Desire.* Cocteau's *Beauty and the Beast* provides a largely surrealistic version of this motif. In fact, a surrealistic undercurrent could be claimed for all the films mentioned above. As always, questions of influence are difficult, but it seems that Van Allsburg's stranger is descended from the godly visitors of ancient stories and has some kinship with the extraterrestrial visitors of recent urban legends and the many films and books those legends have inspired.[10]

In the undercurrent of danger and the irrationality of the premise we sense the surrealist dream developing within *The Stranger.* The strange creatures that invade ordinary lives in Ernst's *Une semaine de bonté* are perhaps gently echoed by the kindly, but indisputably supernatural, presence of the stranger in Van Allsburg's book. The lovely yet realistically ordinary depiction of a gorgeously autumnal rural world serves, however, to deemphasize the surrealistic aspect of this quiet fantasy.[11]

The two dimensions of Chris Van Allsburg's work that I have discussed here—surrealism and strangely-enough fantasy—can be found in all of his books to varying degrees. Because Van Allsburg's surrealism is manifested mostly in his images and the strangely-enough fantasy is evident primarily in his narratives, these two aspects of his work are largely complementary and do not conflict. Both surrealism and the popular traditions of the strange tale provide opportunities to show that the extraordinary resides in the ordinary and vice versa. Surrealism and the weird tale constitute two different but related ways that dreams intrude on everyday life, and Van Allsburg has learned lessons from both of these living traditions to create picture books that continue to fascinate parent-child teams of readers.

NOTES

1. It may seem odd to speak of the tradition established in the name of an avant-garde style of art whose founding practitioners passionately declared themselves to be antitraditional, but it is undeniable that surrealism established stances and styles that have been continued and developed. By speaking of a tradition I am referring to the continuance of some of the ideas and forms of masters such as Magritte and Ernst in the contemporary works of artist-writers such as Van Allsburg.

2. Giorgio de Chirico, with his "metaphysical paintings," could be considered a forerunner of rather than a participant in the surrealist movement. Many of his "surrealistic" works predate Breton's founding of the movement. Chirico is one of those who did not like the term *surrealism* and did not consider himself a surrealist.

3. A large subject I cannot adequately address here is the important ways surrealist artists were themselves influenced by nineteenth-century children's picture books. It has been persuasively argued, for instance, that Max Ernst's *Une semaine de bonté* was influenced by Lewis Carroll's *Alice* books and their Tenniel illustrations (Wilson, 364–71).

4. I wish to make clear that my adoption of Colby's title as the label for a genre of popular pseudo-nonfiction should not be taken as an unqualified tribute to the literary quality of his work. Certainly there was nothing particularly original about what he put together. Collections such as Colby's had been published before—for example R. DeWitt Miller's *Impossible: Yet It Happened* (1947). Miller's book purported to be a study of the paranormal, a claim that was to be repeated by scores of authors who contributed to the paranormal publishing industry that mushroomed in the 1970s and still prospers. A recent series of such collections by Robert Ellis Cahill sells well at various "spooky" tourist spots in New England. The roots of all this can be traced back to the nineteenth century. The "high" tradition of literary polish and sophistication in the spooky tale was advanced by such masters as Charles Dickens, Edgar Allan Poe, and Lafcadio Hearn—but more important to the development of Colby's pseudo-true journalistic tales were the cults of the supernatural encouraged by such things as the early experiments in photography that involved the use of multiple exposures to insert ghosts and faeries into "true" photographs. Such hoaxes and wishful musings have been rife in the flying-saucer and Loch Ness–monster subgenres as well. The superiority of Colby to DeWitt and others of that sort lies in the conciseness of his tale telling. Colby's *Strangely Enough* maintained a long popularity, I suspect, largely because its brief accounts spare the reader the often pompous machinery of the typical paranormal author's explanation of his "field of research." Colby's stories, which have had numerous reprintings, are unencumbered folktales and provide the kind of pleasure any good story affords.

5. It could be argued that the more self-conscious storytelling style of Rod Serling, for instance, kept his published short stories from lingering in the mind with the peculiar aura of plausibility that inheres in Colby's tales. Serling's style exhibited rhetorical effects that signaled he was weaving fictions. Serling did, however, achieve a wide audience for his bizarre stories, especially once he established his type of tale in the medium of television. Serling's narratives seem to fill a different sort of niche in the popular imagination than do Colby's. With Serling we always knew that he was taking us into an artificial realm known as the "Twilight Zone," but with Colby the extraordinary events seemed to be things that happened to genuine, though only sketchily characterized, ordinary people with whom Colby had talked. Weird-tale television innovation of the 1990s took a turn more in Colby's direction with the wildly popular *The X Files* program in which journalistic treatment, ordinary characters, and fragmented plots attempt to give the episodes a nonfictional tone. *The X Files* catch phrase, "the truth is out there," is parallel to the unresolved ending motif that characterizes Colby's tales. The surprisingly popular cult film *The Blair Witch Project* could also be discussed as a strangely-enough project.

6. It is a remarkable feature of journalistic coverage of urban legends that such coverage always results in the further spreading of the legend, even when the journalist is

attempting to debunk the tale. Published versions are inevitably disseminated informally through oral retellings. (The spread of the Internet has also made e-mail retellings a major factor.) Oral dissemination is often accentuated in tourist destinations by the efforts of tour-group leaders who seize upon any and all anecdotes that might entertain their customers. In Hawaii tour guides have gained wide audiences for their versions of such tales. On walking tours, the on-site nature of the tale telling enhances the strangely-enough effect of a story by adding the tangibility of observable buildings, streets, and landscape elements. Even when the conductors of these tours are academically trained scholars, the tales are seldom described as folk legends. It is much more fun for both teller and listener to subscribe to a strange-but-true approach to the material. Further, local tales are seldom related to larger archetypal motifs. For example, the reported tendency of Hawaii's Madame Pele, the volcano goddess, to hitchhike and then disappear from the car is never linked to the widespread legend of the "vanishing hitchhiker," which has been discussed by Jan Harold Brunvand in several of his books. The desire to consider the strange tale as possibly true tends to routinely overwhelm any attempt to debunk the tale. Brunvand, in fact, presents extensive evidence to show that debunkings always serve to further the distribution of the tale (153).

7. The bull terrier that first appeared in *The Garden of Abdul Gasazi* developed into something of a game Van Allsburg plays with his loyal fans. This game involves the reappearance of the bull terrier in book after book; in many of the books the distinctive dog makes his appearance in an obscure corner of only one picture. This odd and amusing practice serves to link Van Allsburg's books to one another. The bull terrier can be found in every one of the picture books discussed in this chapter, as well as in subsequent picture books published after this essay was written. The artist confesses to having enjoyed this find-me exercise (Ruello, 169). This use of a repeated motif, which in popular culture could be called a "running gag," could also be viewed as yet another resemblance to surrealist practice. Magritte, especially, is famed for the repeated appearances of such motifs as chess pieces, harness bells, and men in bowler hats. Van Allsburg's overall opus can be viewed as a unified body of work that includes a playful weaving in and out of this pointless but interesting signature motif; this element of play in serious art is a hallmark of much modernist art influenced by surrealism. The inclination toward playfulness is a key element in Van Allsburg's embrace of both popular culture and surrealism.

8. The value of noticing the strangely-enough plot of *The Garden of Abdul Gasazi* is amply testified to by the misinterpretations of plot action that are fallen into by Peter Neumeyer in a recent article on Van Allsburg that appeared in *Children's Literature Association Quarterly*. Neumeyer insists upon oversimplifying the story by making it into a case of the protagonist-fell-asleep-and-dreamed-an-adventure-and-then-woke-up ploy so common in children's books. It is, however, obviously the case that the boy wakes up and has the encounter with Gasazi in a waking state. After the adventure he returns to the house, missing the telltale hat. For the dream plot to be operative, the boy would have to be shown waking up at the end of the story. The strangely-enough plot provides a way of understanding the bizarreness of the tale without resorting to the unpersuasive leap to the it-was-just-a-dream explanation

that Neumeyer felt he needed to give. In general, Neumeyer's article is flawed by his desire to render Van Allsburg's books as if they were coded messages rather than works of art. Because of Neumeyer's quest for "visual literacy," he fails to do justice to the magic and mystery of Van Allsburg's picture books.

9. This plot bears some resemblance to the plots of the many Japanese Noh plays in which a person from the particular place tells a tale of an earlier time. As in Van Allsburg's story, the teller is eventually discovered to be the character whose woes are being recounted. In Noh plays this tale teller is often a ghost.

10. The list of books and films cited here indicates a continuing theme in popular culture, in which Van Allsburg's *The Stranger* has played a part. Several of the films mentioned postdate Van Allsburg's book and are obviously not considered influences on Van Allsburg. Because the theme of the godlike stranger is so ancient and pervasive, it would be difficult to establish a sequence of influences.

11. The seasonal feeling of *The Stranger* is one of its especially attractive features. I can recall no other picture book more effective at rendering autumn and the harvest time. Van Allsburg's technique of painstakingly laying on tiny unblended lines using pastel provides him with excellent means to realize the bright subtleties of autumn colors. His attention to details—such as individual blades of grass in the foreground, separate dots for leaves in middle-ground trees, strokes suggestive of the grain of wooden floorboards, and attractively plausible stylizations to represent distant elements—results in a book that seems to love the look of its subject. Van Allsburg creates strong sculptural effects in several of the pictures in *The Stranger*, such as the soup-serving scene and the pumpkin-loading scene. For the most part, however, we are not compelled to enter the pictorial space as we are in *The Garden of Abdul Gasazi*. The images in *The Stranger* are separated from the audience by a haze of seasonal romance. The viewer is happy to step back and contemplate the seasonal display.

WORKS CITED

Breton, Andre. *Manifestoes of Surrealism*. Ann Arbor: University of Michigan Press, 1969.

Brunvand, Jan Harold, *The Vanishing Hitchhiker: American Urban Legends and Their Meanings*. New York: Norton, 1981. (Other Brunvand books include *The Baby Train, The Choking Doberman, Curses! Boiled Again*, and *The Mexican Pet*.)

Cahill, Robert Ellis. *New England's Things That Go Bump in the Night*. Peabody, MA: Chandler-Smith, 1989. (Other Cahill works include *New England's Visitors from Outer Space* and *New England's Witches and Wizards*.)

Colby, C. B. *Strangely Enough!* New York: Sterling, 1959.

Ernst, Max. *Une semaine de bonté*. 1934. Reprint. New York: Dover, 1976.

Heinlein, Robert. *Stranger in a Strange Land*. New York: Putnam's, 1961.

Helprin, Mark. *Swan Lake*. Illus. Chris Van Allsburg. Boston: Houghton Mifflin, 1989. (This is the first in Helprin's series of novels featuring strange and gorgeous illustrations by Van Allsburg. Helprin and Van Allsburg seem to be attempting to create illustrated fantasy novels that are as artistically interesting as children's picture books while having the "weight" of novelistic form. Fans of Van Allsburg's picture books may, however, regret that these lovely, though perhaps too weighty productions, along with other interesting illustration assignments, seem to have distracted Van Allsburg from his former habit of regularly producing picture books.)

Hubert, Renee Riese. *Surrealism and the Book*. Berkeley: University of California Press, 1988.

Langer, Susanne K. *Feeling and Form*. New York: Scribner's, 1953.

Lautréamont, Isidore Ducasse. *Les chants de Maldoror*. Trans. Alexis Lykiard. New York: Thomas Y. Crowell, 1972.

Miller, R. DeWitt. *Impossible Yet It Happened!* New York: Ace, 1947.

Murray, Peter, and Linda Murray. *A Dictionary of Art and Artists*. New York: Penguin, 1959.

Neumeyer, Peter. "How Picture Books Mean: The Case of Chris Van Allsburg." *Children's Literature Association Quarterly* 15, No. 1 (1990): 2–8.

Ruello, Catharine. "Chris Van Allsburg Interview." In *Something About the Author*. Ed. Anne Commire. Detroit: Gale Research, 1989: 160–72.

Russell, John. Review of *The Wreck of the Zephyr* by Chris Van Allsburg. *New York Times Book Review* 5 (June 1983): 34.

Serling, Rod. *From the Twilight Zone*. Garden City, NY: Doubleday, 1960.

Van Allsburg, Chris. *Ben's Dream*. Boston: Houghton Mifflin, 1982.

———. *The Garden of Abdul Gasazi*. Boston: Houghton Mifflin, 1979.

———. *Jumanji*. Boston: Houghton Mifflin, 1979.

———. *The Mysteries of Harris Burdick*. Boston: Houghton Mifflin, 1984.

———. *The Polar Express*. Boston: Houghton Mifflin, 1985.

———. *The Stranger*. Boston: Houghton Mifflin, 1885.

———. *The Wreck of the Zephyr*. Boston: Houghton Mifflin, 1983.

———. *The Z Was Zapped*. Boston: Houghton Mifflin, 1987.

Wilson, Sarah. "Max Ernst and England." In *Max Ernst: A Retrospective*. Ed. Werner Spies. Munich: Prestel-Verlag, 1991: 363–72.

OTHER WORKS OF INTEREST

Cummings, Pat, ed. *Talking with Artists*. New York: Macmillan, 1991. (Van Allsburg is one of the artists interviewed.)

Van Allsburg, Chris. *Bad Day at Riverbend*. Boston: Houghton Mifflin, 1995.

———. *The Sweetest Fig*. Boston: Houghton Mifflin, 1993.

———. *The Window's Broom*. Boston: Houghton Mifflin, 1992.

———. *The Wretched Stone*. Boston: Houghton Mifflin, 1991.